ENDORSEME

The great privilege of the Christian life is to discover how to live in the realm of God's glory. The apostle Paul said that because of sin we *"have fallen short of the glory of God"* (Romans 3:23). In other words, it was in our original design to live and thrive in that glory. Sin only temporarily delayed God's plan, as the blood of Jesus restores us to our original design. To hunger for, and only be satisfied by, the manifested presence of Jesus is written in our spiritual DNA. His presence is what makes the rest of life purposeful. In a practical sense, the seamless connection with the glory is realized through our relationship with the Holy Spirit. Only His glory can satisfy the appetite of the believing believer.

God has purposed for the whole earth to be filled with His glory. This was declared after sin entered the world. It is His redemptive plan; it is His desire and commitment—and it will happen. He has chosen to accomplish, at least a portion of that goal, through the co-laboring efforts of His presence-centered people. Such yielded ones have responded to His plan in the same way Isaiah did, by saying, "Here I am! Send me!" That's our privileged assignment, to be people in the presence who carry the presence in whatever sphere we are assigned to.

I have a deep love and admiration for Tommy Evans and his wife, Miriam. I was given the unusual privilege of having a front row seat to their journey, as they attended our school of ministry and Tommy interned with me for a year. Their love for God and their passion for revival are real. And their passion to live in the glory is palpable, affecting all who know them. I am amazed. They continue in this expression of absolute surrender through their lifestyle of purity, passion, and power. They live with the understanding that Jesus deserves nothing less than our all. I am excited to see a generation of lovers of God raised up who value His presence and His glory above everything else.

BILL JOHNSON
Bethel Church, Redding, CA
Author of *Open Heavens* and *Born for Significance*

Nothing compares with the tangible, manifested glory of God. Tommy Evans has experienced what we all long for—Holy Spirit flooding the room, overtaking the atmosphere—and he brings it to us in a manner that invites us to participate. If you find yourself longing to "go deeper, I suggest you dive heart first into His glory.

TIM SHEETS
Oasis Church

Tommy Evans's book *Anointed for Glory* is a must-read. In this book Tommy gives insight, revelation, and practical application through personal experiences as well as a biblical foundation to enable a believer to become carriers of the glory. *Anointed for Glory* makes it very clear what is available for us today. We need a divine encounter that will transform the church and the world. *Anointed for Glory* will help you position yourself for a life-changing encounter with God. We cannot just be containers of God's glory; we must become dispensers of the glory to the world around us. *Anointed for*

Glory will enrich your walk with God and light a fire in your heart to encounter Him in a new and more powerful way.

MARK and PATRICIA ESTES
Apostolic Overseers, North Palm Global Network

Anointed for Glory is a much needed book for the body of Christ or for those who hunger for more of God and may not know how to go about accessing the fire of God that brings the glory. By using Scripture, personal examples, and prayers, this book will help lead you to experience the glory as God has always intended for His people.

STAN AND DEANNA JONES
Lead Pastors, Light in the Wilderness Church
Hardy, Arkansas

Tommy Evans has a right and a responsibility to write about the glory. We have watched his life for over 20 years. No one has studied, pursued, preached, or practiced the glory of God like Tommy and Miriam Evans. Our church is experiencing a new level of presence of Holy Spirit in our meetings and in the community because Tommy and Miriam spent years loving, welcoming, encountering Holy Spirit. This book is an honest and raw journey of one man, one couple, pursuing the presence of God. And they are now bringing God's glory to churches and communities all over the world. The Hennesys love the Evans family. They have honored us well and now God is using them to see the glory of God cover the earth. As you read this book, you will become so hungry for the glory of God and know it is possible to experience it and be carriers of it.

BECKY HENNESY
Co-Pastor, Trinity Church
Founder of the Hennesy Foundation

Anointed for Glory is the holy expression of a heart that refuses to settle for limitations placed on Holy Spirit and a catalyst for high level activity of God. As the Evanses served in our church for 10 years, Tommy and Miriam ignited a culture of expectancy and faith while demonstrating how Jesus has decided to show Himself mighty on behalf of those with courage and hunger to pursue Him. This book records the journey of discovery and the stewardship of anointing. It is a must-read for the new-era church.

JIM HENNESY
Senior Pastor, Trinity Church

I have witnessed the faithful pursuit of God's presence in the life of my husband, Tommy Evans. As his wife, I have seen my husband's desire to search out hidden keys in God's word that prepare us to experience the Glory of the Lord. Tommy's revelation on the Glory has enriched my life, and I am confident that the biblical revelations found in this book will bless an entire generation to be Anointed to carry the Glory of the Lord!

MIRIAM EVANS
Co-Founder of Revival Mandate International
Author of *Glory Miracles*
Co-Author of *Decrees That Unlock Heaven's Power*

This is truly one of the best books on the subject of God's glory that I've ever read. It's informative and inspirational, filled with engaging, systematic Bible teaching and loads of eye-witness testimonies of God's supernatural power in operation. But what sets this book apart is the very thing that makes Tommy Evans unique. As someone who regularly travels and ministers with Tommy, and counts him as a true brother in Christ, I can say without exaggeration that he operates in a legitimate spiritual gift of impartation—that when Tommy prays for people, they receive and experience what he carries. Make no mistake, it's not Tommy imparting something; it's the Holy Spirit using Tommy to impart and ignite a deep hunger for God's glory that brings you into a dynamic collision with a God-encounter. This book is not meant to be merely read; it's meant to be felt and experienced. You will be deeply provoked, chapter after chapter, as you read about the Bible expressions of God's glorious presence, and how they are available to taste today. *Anointed for Glory* is not for someone chasing cheap thrills, zings or spiritual parlor tricks; this book is for those whose hearts burn with the cry of Moses towards the Holy One: "Please, Show Me Your Glory!" Prepare yourself: He will respond.

LARRY SPARKS, MDIV.
Publisher, *Destiny Image*
Author, *Pentecostal Fire: Your Supernatural Inheritance*
Co-founder, LM Sparks Ministries

ANOINTED
FOR
GLORY

IMPARTATION TO MOVE WITH GOD'S MANIFEST PRESENCE

TOMMY EVANS

DESTINY IMAGE® PUBLISHERS, INC.

P.O. Box 310, Shippensburg, PA 17257-0310

"Publishing cutting-edge prophetic resources to supernaturally empower the body of Christ"

This book and all other Destiny Image and Destiny Image Fiction books are available at Christian bookstores and distributors worldwide.

For more information on foreign distributors, call 717-532-3040.

Reach us on the Internet: www.destinyimage.com.

ISBN 13 TP: 978-0-7684-7443-5
ISBN 13 eBook: 978-0-7684-7444-2
ISBN 13 HC: 978-0-7684-7446-6
ISBN 13 LP: 978-0-7684-7445-9

For Worldwide Distribution, Printed in the U.S.A.
1 2 3 4 5 6 7 8 / 27 26 25 24 23

DEDICATION

I want to dedicate this book to my Lord and friend, Holy Spirit. You have always been such an inspiration and encouragement to me, which makes me eternally grateful. Thank you for always pursuing me, despite my flaws and imperfections, while revealing Your love for me. Your love, devotion, patience, and kindness toward me empower me daily to live from a place of victory and grace. I am so honored to not only call You my Lord but also my friend. I love You.

ACKNOWLEDGMENTS

My Beloved Wife

I want to thank my incredible wife, Miriam, for always being by my side and loving me unconditionally. You really are the woman of my dreams. I love you.

My Beloved Children

I want to honor all of my amazing kids. You make my heart full in so many ways. Your love, gifts, and personal attributes reflect Jesus so beautifully. Daddy loves you.

My Covenant Friend

I want to thank my dear friend Larry Sparks and the entire Destiny Image team for believing in both Miriam and me. Larry, as I have told you before, God gave you to us, and for that I am thankful. You truly are a covenant friend.

Family and Friends

I want to thank my extended family and friends. Your love and encouragement inspire us to reach further and further every day.

Spiritual Mothers and Fathers

I want to thank Bill and Beni Johnson for being such an example to me over the years to make God's presence the priority in life. Your heart for Jesus is contagious.

I also want to thank Cindy and Mike Jacobs, Patricia King, Jim and Becky Hennesy, Dan and Marti Duke, as well as Stan and Deanna Jones for imparting to me over the years. Your love, devotion, and discipleship have shaped me into the man I am today. You all have played such an integral role in our lives. I am eternally grateful to all of you and love you deeply.

CONTENTS

FOREWORD

BY PATRICIA KING

We are all created to experience God's glory, and everyone who has received Jesus Christ as Lord and Savior can. Not all do, but all can, because the presence of Christ in believers is the very hope of glory. By nature, we were made for the glory, and we are by nature hungry for the glory.

I love the example of Moses, found in Exodus 33:9-11, where he is seen to regularly approach God in the tent of meeting in the wilderness. Every time he chose to meet with God, the "pillar of cloud" (God's glory presence) would descend and the Lord would speak to Moses face to face, just as a man speaks to his friend. Whenever I read this, fresh hunger stirs in my heart to experience God like that too.

Although Moses had regular encounters in the presence, he longed for more. In verse 18 we find Moses desperately crying out for more: "Show me Your glory!" Deep cries unto deep. God heard the deep groanings of Moses's heart and granted him the revelation and experience of being hidden in Jesus the Savior as the glory of God passed by.

The glory of God is a massive subject to explore because in essence His glory is the fullness of all that He is and all that He has. The glory is the fullness of Jesus Himself. It will take us all eternity to explore the depth, width, height, and breadth of His glory. We as believers are invited to a never-ending journey of encountering one degree of God's glory upon another. If you have not begun this journey yet, this book will most likely become a revelatory portal through which you can access the promises and the realities of personal glory encounters.

Imagine yourself experiencing wave after wave of the tangible, weighty presence of God's holiness, love, joy, mercy, and peace. Think of the possibility of accessing angelic glory or seeing the manifestations of miracles, signs, and wonders in and through your life. Can you see yourself, like Moses and the elders of Israel, ascending into heaven and eating and drinking on sapphire streets before the presence of God (see Exodus 24:9-10)? Does the thought of embracing these types of encounters excite you? If so, you are reading the right book!

So many believers in this day have held to a form of godliness but denied the power (see 2 Timothy 3:5), but we do not find a powerless gospel in the Scriptures. We are invited to experience the Lord in His fullness. We have been granted access into the holiest of all, to stand in His very glory presence through the blood of Jesus Christ.

Having therefore, brethren, boldness to enter into the holiest by the blood of Jesus, by a new and living way, which he hath consecrated for us, through the veil, that is to say, his flesh; and having an high priest over the house of God; let us draw near with a true heart in full assurance of faith, having our hearts sprinkled from an evil conscience, and our bodies washed with pure water (Hebrews 10:19-22 KJV).

In Christ Jesus our Lord: in whom we have boldness and access with confidence by the faith of him (Ephesians 3:11-12 KJV).

Tommy and Miriam Evans are authentic and upright carriers and ministers of Kingdom glory. As seasoned revivalists, they have been obedient to the call of God on their lives and have been willing to take risks to trust Him to manifest His presence, power, and majesty. Everywhere they go to minister, the glory manifests—it is their expectation.

In *Anointed for Glory*, Tommy Evans practically and with refreshing simplicity teaches important insights on the glory and how to step into "presence encounters." As I read this book, I was refreshed in my hunger for more of God, and you will be too.

May I encourage you to personally stir up fresh hunger for the Lord and glory encounters in Him? If you hunger and thirst for righteousness, you shall be filled. It's time to be filled to overflowing with more of Him. Glory!

FOREWORD

BY CINDY JACOBS

Tommy Evans has hit the mark with his new book, *Anointed for Glory.* He verbalizes what is in the heart of God's people right at this moment: a desperation to know Him more.

Revival and awakening are in the air! Thousands are turning to Christ but they don't know how to walk out what is happening in their lives. Tommy is both transparent and vulnerable about the frustrations and challenges both he and his lovely wife, Miriam, experienced in trying to reach out for more of God.

More God! Those two words are the cry that I heard from people in revivals across the world. Mike and I were deeply involved in the Argentine revival and I credit that phrase from that time period. As

you read these pages, it will become very clear to you that from the depths of their beings, this couple is crying out those two words.

Tommy gives us keys to why they are seeing the outstanding results of experiencing the glory of God in their personal lives and on a corporate level—they worked hard for it. They made a prayer plan and stuck to it: they searched the Word and soaked in the presence of God.

One doesn't become more intimate with Him by being lazy. One seeks for God and His fullness.

They encountered resistance. Tommy wrote, "Sometimes in life you will discover that the greatest opposition you face will be at the point of your greatest breakthrough!" So true! I have experienced that myself. When God is getting ready to push you through to a new level, it may seem like all hell breaks out before all heaven breaks through! This is where people often get discouraged and quit. They either don't want more of God very badly, or they let the opposition stop them in their tracks.

I often say, if you are going into your promised land to occupy and there are no giants, you are only a tourist. However, when Satan comes at you as a roaring lion, roar back! When you resist him, he will flee (or, in my paraphrase, run in absolute terror).

Tommy and Miriam had to make some decisions to go to the next level. It was tough, and whenever one does such a thing, chaos can break out. Oftentimes the glory is preceded by chaos. Don't let that deter you! Just take it as a sign that God is getting ready to do awesome things in your life and you are moving into a new season.

If you are hungry for God's manifest presence and you want to experience His glory, this book is for you! If you are seeking God's will to go to a new level, this book is for you! It will wreck you in a good way and help you become more on fire and radical each and every day.

Open these pages and begin your supernatural adventure now!

CINDY JACOBS
Generals International

CHAPTER 1

REVELATION OF GLORY

*For the earth will be filled with the knowledge of
the glory of the Lord, as the waters cover the sea.*
—HABAKKUK 2:14 NKJV

It was around October 2002 when I found myself extremely frustrated, to be quite honest. Miriam and I had only been married for two years, and we decided to move to the hills of northeast Arkansas. Yes, I'm sure you are already asking yourself, "Why Arkansas?" Well, I am originally from Arkansas, and I thought it would be a great idea to take my new wife—who, mind you, is a city girl—back to my hometown to go on this great big adventure of acculturating her to country life. My sweet little wife was willing to make the move because she had already decided in her heart that she would follow her man to the uttermost parts of the earth!

After settling into our new home, we decided that we needed to get plugged into a local church. It ended up being an Assemblies of God church that I had attended when I was in my younger years. Immediately upon diving into our new church, the pastors saw a higher calling that honestly Miriam and I did not even knew existed! They began to call out things in us that quite frankly made absolutely no sense to either of us.

Why didn't it make sense to us, you might ask? Well, Miriam and I were quite the pair. We had just come out of a life of sin, and honestly we were two hot messes to say the least! We had decided to really give our lives to Jesus just two years prior, and we were still trying to work some things out in our marriage and personally with the Lord. So when our pastors began to call out the good that they saw God doing in our lives, it brought quite a shock. We both began to ask ourselves things like, "How can God use people like us with so many mistakes?" as well as thoughts like, "Really, God? You've called us to be ministers of the gospel?"

I want to interject something here before I go further. You need to make sure that wherever you are on your journey with God, you get around people who will see what God sees in you and will call you up higher! If you're not where you want to be in your life, it might be because you are in a boat with the wrong people! Do yourself a favor and find people who believe in you and are willing to love you enough to call out the gold in you.

So back to my frustration that I mentioned earlier at the beginning of my story. About six months after our arrival at our new church, our pastors invited us to become youth pastors of the church and also asked me if I would be willing to lead worship on Sunday nights. So with great hesitancy and trepidation, we accepted this new position. Miriam and I were off to a really great start. We had Bible studies, youth activities at our home, parent meetings, and youth-activated mission trips that really stretched us as leaders. Even though this was new to us, we felt like we were really going somewhere in life and felt a sense of purpose. Yet after quite some time with all the right church activities in place, something still seemed to be missing in our lives.

As time went on, I began to hear my excited wife tell me all of these amazing God encounters she was having. She would tell me how she heard God speak to her and would often share dreams of angelic activity with me. I remember specifically when she had an open vision of an angel sitting at the foot of our bed and the weighty presence of God filling our room. Great stories, right? Well, for her it was amazing, but for me not so much. Why, you might ask? Well, since you really want to know, it was because none of that God activity was happening to me! In fact, when this angelic encounter happened, I was dead asleep! I would be a dishonest man if I did not mention how frustrated I was that I had not encountered God or even heard Him speak to me personally. I was happy for Miriam but frustrated for me, to say the least. I began to wonder if God even liked me. As my frustration grew, Miriam continued to have amazing, ongoing encounters with God, which really brought a lot of encouragement to her.

FRUSTRATION TURNS TO DESPERATION

I really wanted to encounter God and I desperately wanted to hear Him. I remember pleading with God, almost begging to at least hear Him speak. My desperate cries quite honestly sounded more like complaining and did not amount to much, for the most part.

I remember getting up many times and asking God to speak to me, but I only got dead silence in return! Nothing! Nada! Zilch! I even tried beating my bed with my fists and shouting out to God, "I must hear You!" Again, silence!

I didn't realize at the time that through my desperation, God was cultivating my heart and preparing me for His divine purpose and ongoing encounters with Him. One of my spiritual fathers, Bill Johnson, says it best: "Prayer doesn't change God's heart; it changes yours." The fallow ground of my heart was being tilled up and held by the Master as I continued to cry out desperately for the more of God. The capacity of my heart was being transformed so that I could carry what God was about to do.

CONSISTENCY IS THE KEY

After reading much of the Bible, Miriam and I began to realize that if the Bible is true, then according to the Bible there must be power in prayer. As we received this new revelation about the power of prayer, we decided that we would make daily prayer a priority instead of it just being a casual thing. With our daughter Kathryn being only two years old at the time, Miriam and I decided that we would take turns watching her while the other prayed. Every day we separately and privately would go into our room, lock the door behind us, and spend consistent time with God. I personally kept going in daily even though my time with God didn't seem to amount to a whole lot. I decided in my heart that I was going to pursue Jesus whether I encountered Him or not. I knew in my heart that the price that Jesus paid on the cross for my sins was enough for me and He was worthy of my worship. Now, instead of pleading and begging, I just worshiped as I went daily into my bedroom to pray.

Then it happened. After months of just worshiping and praying for others as they came to mind, I suddenly felt a weighty presence fill my bedroom. Suddenly I found myself caught up in the emotions of God toward me. I felt His immense love for me. I've never felt such a weighty love in my entire life. It was as though love itself had just exploded in my room!

God baptized me in His love that day. I was keenly immersed in God, to say the least. This overwhelming feeling led me to tears and, of course, to my knees. I began to weep uncontrollably as the love of God penetrated my entire soul. It was like liquid love flooding every ounce of my being. I wept with tears of love and joy for several hours. As I wept, God was communicating with me Spirit to spirit. I didn't want to leave this place with God. I honestly wanted to stay there forever. To be quite honest, it is actually hard for me to fully describe here in words. I think the best and most accurate way to describe it was that Jesus walked into the room and my entire being knew it! Jesus came with His manifest presence! I believe that what I was experiencing was an aspect of the glory of God.

Later in this book, I will do my best to describe different aspects of the glory as well as give you personal experiences, a biblical basis, and how to carry what I call *the glory*. But first I would like to lay a backdrop with two prophetic dreams that I had, a prophetic word for the *now* and an encounter that I had, to set the stage for the rest of the book.

I believe this series of prophetic events opened up a realm of revelation into the glory that would later set me up to receive divine impartation to carry the glory. Keep in mind as you read this book that the revelation we receive from God sets us up to receive divine impartation from God, which results in the manifestation of the glory of God.

ANGELIC ENCOUNTER DREAM: MESSAGE OF GLORY, 2005

Isn't it just like God to bring you so much encouragement at some of the darkest times? If you're going through a tough time right now, I want to encourage you that God has not left you! He is with you and is at work at this very moment even if you can't see it yet! So be encouraged!

One of the most profound and powerful encounters I have ever had is the one I'm about to share with you. It was the year 2005, and we had just moved back to Texas from Arkansas. Honestly, Miriam and I were going through a hard time, and we really needed God to break in. We were experiencing some great resistance, and the enemy of our destiny did not want us going to the next level. Sometimes in life, you will discover that the greatest opposition you face will be at the point of your greatest breakthrough! That is exactly what was happening to us.

I remember going to bed and falling asleep relatively quickly. Immediately upon falling asleep, it was as though I stepped into another realm. It was a God realm! In this very vivid experience, I had my first angelic encounter. An angel came to me and took me to three different places. The first place he took me was a wall of Hebraic scripture. As I looked at the Hebraic scripture, I suddenly realized that I understood what it meant. It was the prophecy in Ezekiel 43, and it was all about the glory returning to the temple. As I finished reading this prophecy, the angel took me to the mount of transfiguration. As I stood there, I saw the scene in Matthew

17 taking place. I saw Jesus and the glory resting upon Him. This glory manifested as a bright light that actually was blinding to me in this vision. As I stood there in this blinding light, I heard the Holy Spirit say, "I am about to transfigure the face of My church. They will be transformed to be carriers of My glory."

Again, the angel took me to a third place. This place was a large stadium-type arena. As I was led through the front door, upon entering I saw world leaders on their knees, not able to stand, and I noticed that there was a great multitude slain under the power of God. None of the people could stand because of the weight of glory in the room. As I watched, I noticed that the people who were slain were the saved and the unsaved. A world leader crawled toward me and asked me, "Do you see them? Do you see them?"

I immediately asked him, "See what?"

He said, "The angels. They are everywhere."

When he said that, immediately my eyes were open in the spirit realm, and I saw a myriad of angels that were ushering in the glory of God. When I saw this, I too was slain under the power of God. The weight of glory was so strong that I could not stand up. I lay there with a multitude of others. The person on my left was saved and the person on my right was not saved, but we were all caught up in the weightiness of God's immense love. It was absolutely glorious.

Upon waking from this encounter I heard the Holy Spirit say:

This coming move of God will come with the greatest manifestation of glory that humanity has ever seen. This coming glory of God will be so great that no one will be able to speak against it or refute that it was God. There will be such a display of power that it will shock the earth. This glory will fall on the saved and the unsaved with many coming to Jesus because of it.s

For I heard the Spirit say, "I am about to transfigure the face of the Church so that My glory will be seen upon them."

ENCOUNTER WITH THE FIRE OF GOD, 2011

It was October 2011, and we got a devastating phone call that our dear friends wanted to get a divorce after thirty years of marriage. At the time, Miriam and I owned our own business, so we had the freedom to make quick arrangements to purchase plane tickets to go and see them in an attempt to help save their marriage. As we settled into bed for the night in the mountains of Colorado, I had no idea what was about to happen.

As I lay there in bed pondering on the day, I felt the weighty presence of God fill the room. I sensed that God wanted to show me something, so I decided to just worship Jesus as He entered the room. As I continued to worship, suddenly I felt the tangible presence of God come upon my body. My right hand and arm began to twitch and then my left. My feet began to tremble as I lay there just continuing to worship. As this twitching continued, my whole body began to tremble violently as though I had just touched two hundred and twenty 220 volts of electricity! The crazy thing about the trembling that I was experiencing was that it did not hurt at all. I felt a peace and a sense of holiness that are hard to describe. As this encounter continued, Miriam became fully aware of what was going on. As I shook violently in the bed, I began to prophetically decree what God intended to do in our lives. I began to prophesy things that honestly kind of scared me at the time because I simply didn't have an understanding for them all. This went on for almost three hours!

After this encounter in October, we had no idea that God was actually preparing us for something that would be so catalytic for our lives. The beautiful thing about the Lord is that when He takes hold of you with His holy fire, it's never just to give you a thrill. His encounters that He brings to you and me are always unto something. God took hold of me that night because He knew I would need a fresh anointing for what He was about to ask of us.

That following year, God began to show us that we were stepping into a great transition and it was time to follow Him with abandoned faith. We were extremely comfortable with the lifestyle that we currently had. We made good money and had a great family and a nice little home, but God had a better plan, to say the least. God began to show us very clearly that we were to relocate from Texas to be a part of what He was doing at a church community in Redding, California. God revealed to us that we were to catch the spirit of revival there and go learn from those who were moving in sustained revival glory.

God truly knew what He was doing even though we did not at the time. The fire that God poured out on my life that night in Colorado would prepare me to carry something that I had never carried before. Again, when we encounter the fire of God it is always unto something. I would like to make the proposition that every encounter that we have with the fire of God is what prepares us to carry His weighty glory. In other words, the fire prepares us for *the glory.*

PROPHETIC WORD: ISAIAH 60
MOMENT, OCTOBER 2020

For the last three years, Miriam and I have had the wonderful privilege of sitting on the Apostolic Council of Prophetic Elders with Cindy and Mike Jacobs of Generals International. Every year we gather around the table with apostles and prophets from all around the world, hearing what God has spoken so that we can collectively give a corporate word of the Lord to the nations. God began to reveal to me that the Church at large was entering into an "Isaiah 60 and 61 Moment." I really began to dig deeper into these prophetic passages to get a better understanding of what the Lord was saying to me. Let's look into these two passages together and I will reveal what God began to show me concerning this.

> *The Spirit of the Lord God is upon Me, because the Lord has anointed Me to preach good tidings to the poor; He has sent Me to heal the brokenhearted, to proclaim liberty to the captives, and the opening of the prison to those who are bound; to proclaim the acceptable year of the Lord, and the day of vengeance of our God; to comfort all who mourn, to console those who mourn in Zion, to give them beauty for ashes, the oil of joy for mourning, the garment of praise for the spirit of heaviness; that they may be called trees of righteousness, the planting of the Lord, that He may be glorified* (Isaiah 61:1-3 NKJV).

> *Arise, shine; for your light has come! And the glory of the Lord is risen upon you. For behold, the darkness shall cover the earth, and deep darkness the people; but the Lord will arise over you, and His glory will be seen upon*

you. The Gentiles shall come to your light, and kings to the brightness of your rising (Isaiah 60:1-3 NKJV).

Currently, our nation has been facing racial and political divide, riots in the streets, and a historical global pandemic. Internationally, we are seeing a moral decline, continuous murders, continued drug use, abortion, divorce, wars, and gender confusion. The enemy of our souls has launched a global attack that stands in opposition to God and His children. There is some serious darkness covering the earth, to say the least! The great news is that God is not surprised and He has a plan! I would like to suggest that the plan of God includes you rising in multiplied anointing that carries glory! Now that's good news!

God began to make it very clear to me that the only remedy for the problems that we are facing as a nation and on the earth is revival of glory in the heart of mankind. The Holy Spirit began to show me out of these two passages that God is anointing His people to be carriers of His great glory! We are entering into a season in which God is multiplying His anointing upon us to carry the weightiest manifestation of His glory that we have ever seen! After God spoke to me out of these two passages, a few months later He gave me a prophetic dream to confirm what He was revealing to me concerning this last-days anointing of glory.

PROPHETIC DREAM: CARRIERS OF GLORY, AUGUST 2021

To be honest with you, I don't dream much, but when I do I know the Lord is speaking to me. God wastes nothing. Whether you dream every now and then or you dream often, I recommend writing down those dreams and inviting the Holy Spirit to give you understanding. As I went to bed, I immediately fell asleep into a very vivid and real dream. In the dream, I saw Miriam. Most often when I dream about my wife, I know that the Lord is revealing something to me about His precious bride. I want to encourage you to ask the Holy Spirit to give you a specific dream language so that you can begin to get a greater understanding of what He may be showing you.

So back to my dream. As I was observing Miriam, I noticed she was wearing a huge gold ring on her ring finger that had a Hebrew word written on it. In the dream I knew in my spirit that the Hebrew letters meant *kabod.* Upon waking from the dream, I immediately went and looked up the Hebrew letters, and sure enough the letters spelled *kabod,* which means "my glory"! The Holy Spirit began to show me that He was making a proposal to His precious bride to be carriers of His glory. Come on, somebody! That is great news! What a privilege we have in God's sovereignty—He chooses us to be carriers of His great glory so that Jesus can be fully expressed in the earth! I just want to encourage you to lift up your hands right now and give Jesus thanks!

For the remainder of this book, I will do my best to describe to you what the glory is, the different vehicles that God uses to manifest His glory, how to carry God's glory, and how to release God's glory. This book is not an exhaustive study on *the glory,* but it will provide a biblical basis for it, stories of others in revival history who carried it, and personal testimonies of how God has used both Miriam and me in this manner. My hope is that the rest of this book will create an appetite within your being that will ignite a hunger to be a carrier of glory.

Let's pray:

> *Lord, I ask that You give me a revelation of Your glory. Holy Spirit, will You help me to receive and learn to release Your glory? Help me to be a carrier of Your manifest presence in Jesus's name. Amen.*

CHAPTER 2

SHOW ME YOUR GLORY: THE GLORY DEFINED

If you are reproached for the name of Christ, blessed are you, for the Spirit of glory and of God rests upon you.
—1 PETER 4:14 NKJV

Several years ago I began to hear others in the body of Christ talk about *the glory*. Honestly, at that time I had no idea what that even meant. Through a series of prophetic dreams and encounters, God began to create within me a hunger to know more about *the glory*. One of those dreams included a passage in the book of Hebrews. As I mentioned in the first chapter, I don't dream a lot, but when I do I make it a habit to pay attention.

*Therefore, leaving the discussion of the elementary prin-
ciples of Christ, let us go on to perfection [maturity], not
laying again the foundation of repentance from dead
works and of faith toward God, of the doctrine of bap-
tisms, of laying on of hands, of resurrection of the dead,
and of eternal judgment* (Hebrews 6:1 NKJV).

Upon waking from this dream, I felt like the Holy Spirit was
revealing to me that He has a deep desire to bring the body of
Christ into a greater level of maturity by revealing deeper mysteries
of the glory realm.

Now you may be asking, "Really, Tommy? Do you really
believe God is giving you some kind of new revelation?" No, not
at all! But what I am suggesting here is that God does bring us
into encounters to unmask what His powerful Word has already
made available. Encounters with God unveil deep mysteries of
what He has said so that we can better understand what He is
doing. Jesus said, "I only do what I see My Father doing" (see
John 5:19). I believe that Jesus was able to see what the Father
was doing because He saw it first through divine encounter. We
must remember that Jesus is our model for all aspects of life and
ministry. If Jesus positioned Himself for ongoing encounters, then
so must we.

In the second book of Corinthians, Paul described a heavenly
encounter in which he heard words he didn't feel allowed to even
speak about. God was showing him deep mysteries (see 2 Corinthians 12:2-4). The Bible is our standard for New Testament
Christianity and declares to us all that God has made available
for us. The Scripture lays a precedent for ongoing encounters and
gives us permission to pursue them. Because of the shed blood of

Jesus and the Holy Spirit dwelling within us, you and I have access to open-door encounters with the heavenly realm.

We must take this amazing opportunity and become people who move from milk to meat—babies to mature sons and daughters of the Most High. It's the glory of God to conceal a matter, but the glory of kings to search it out! (See Proverbs 25:2.) It is time that we begin to search out the deep things of God so we can partner with Him to see His glory revealed throughout the whole earth.

Now back to our discussion of *the glory*. Again, I heard this term used many times and no one was really explaining what it meant or how it was expressed. To be quite honest, it seemed a bit mystical and far from reach at the time. My hope is that you and I can journey together to demystify the term *glory* and step into a greater understanding so that you can carry it and release it everywhere you go.

As I began to ask the Holy Spirit what the term *glory* and *glory realm* meant, He took me straight to His Word! Let's take what the Bible says about the glory of the Lord.

> *And it came to pass, when the priests came out of the holy place, that the cloud filled the house of the Lord, so that the priests could not continue ministering because of the cloud; for the glory of the Lord filled the house of the Lord* (1 Kings 8:10-11 NKJV).

> *And he [Moses] said, "Please, show me Your glory." Then He said, "I will make all My goodness pass before you, and I will proclaim the name of the Lord before you. I will be gracious to whom I will be gracious, and I*

will have compassion on whom I will have compassion"
(Exodus 33:18-19 NKJV).

For the earth will be filled with the knowledge of the
glory of the Lord, as the waters cover the sea (Habakkuk
2:14 NKJV).

As we look into the glory, I want to make sure every reader understands that I am not creating some extra-biblical idea here or putting anything whatsoever above Jesus dying on the cross for us or the power of His resurrection. Nor am I exalting some idea above the precious work of the Holy Spirit. What I do want you to consider, however, is that the Scriptures referenced above are all out of the Old Testament, which I believe is an inferior covenant to the New Covenant found in Jesus Christ.

I want us to remember that because of Jesus our Savior, we have become partakers of a better covenant. My question is, if that's true, then why is it that most of the New Testament church today has not experienced some of what the Old Testament believers partook in?

Why is it that much of the church today has become full of programs, man-made agendas, dead religion, and scheduled time clocks instead of a place where the glory of the Lord manifests in our midst? Why has most of the church today become so irrelevant that we are not attractive to a lost and dying world? If I were to be totally honest, I believe it is because we have simply settled for less as a church at large. We've settled for the status quo instead of the presence and power of the Holy Spirit. We've settled for yesterday's glory, making the stories of the Bible something that we just reference in our polished sermons instead of pressing into a demonstration of power and great glory. This must not be!

Think about it. The patriarchs of the Bible and the early church experienced clouds of glory, fire, manna on the ground, a burning bush, miracles, healings, shadow healings, lightnings, smoke, bodies of water splitting, water coming out of a rock, resurrections from the dead, signs, wonders, and great glory.

Why is it that they experienced all of that and most of the church gets offended the minute someone gets hit by the power of the Spirit and filled with holy laughter? It doesn't make sense to me that an inferior covenant or a former move of God would provide superior blessings. We must press into the greater prophetic promise that is found in the book of Haggai.

> *The glory of this latter temple shall be greater than the former* (Haggai 2:9 NKJV).

This passage tells us that there is more! There is *greater glory* available for you and me! You and I have a huge responsibility to press into the *greater glory* or we will never see it manifested in the earth. God is looking for those who will press into greater measures of His precious presence and power! Let's take a closer look at what the glory is and isn't so that we have the tools necessary to explore the *greater* that God has made available to us.

The Hebrew word for *glory* in the above Scriptures is *kabod*, which means "glory, honor, abundance, riches, and splendor." The root word is *kabad*, which means "weighty, heavy, glorious, or great." I would like to suggest that *the glory* is God's goodness, abundance, riches, and splendor being made manifest through the weightiness of His presence. It's like God showing up and everything in your triune being becoming fully aware and attentive. It is God there, front and center, and you know it! It is the presence and power of Jesus being made known.

EXPLANATION OF THE GLORY

I want to take a moment and show you a few things that God has shown me through biblical understanding and personal revelation, as well as gleaning from spiritual fathers and mothers who move in the glory. In order for us to have a better understanding of *the glory,* we must first understand something very important about the Holy Spirit.

The first thing that we need to understand concerning the Holy Spirit is that He is the third person of the Godhead. He is not a force, an "it," or just some wonderful experience. I would like to suggest here that He is *not* the glory. He is a Person. He is the Spirit of Christ. He is Christ unlimited in the heart of believers. I like what Pastor Benny Hinn says: "When Jesus walked on this earth, He was limited, and when He ascended, sending the Holy Spirit, He became unlimited." The Holy Spirit is our comforter, our teacher, our companion, our encouragement, our friend, and our Lord. He is the one who sanctifies us and teaches us all things.

The Holy Spirit is the one who reveals Jesus to us and makes Him known to us. The Holy Spirit is the prophetic spirit who shows us things to come and reveals our purpose. He is not "a power"; He is "power" itself. He is the *dunamis* of heaven. We must come to fully know this precious gift that we have been given so that we can gain a better understanding of *the glory* and how to carry it.

The second thing I would like to suggest to you is that *the glory* is not a person but the presence of the Person of the Holy Spirit. I would agree with Pastor John Kilpatrick, who explains the glory as an atmosphere or environment that God brings when He chooses to manifest Himself in a given situation. I like how

Ruth Ward Heflin describes the glory in her book *Glory*: "As air is the atmosphere of the earth, glory is the atmosphere of heaven."[1]

The glory is the atmosphere or environment of the Holy Spirit! His glory is His very presence being made known! And when this happens, good things take place! The point that I want you to get is that *the glory* is the realm of the triune God being made manifest through the Holy Spirit.

This being stated, does that mean that this glory is always being manifested? Not necessarily. We all know that God is omnipresent, which means He is everywhere at all times. I think we can all agree on that. But we must come to know and understand that God does not manifest or make His presence known everywhere. We see this both in biblical history and in revival history. In the 1990s, God manifested Himself in places like Brownsville, Toronto, Brazil, and Argentina, resulting in historical revivals. These places became specific hotspots where God was choosing to manifest His great glory. The glory of God's manifest presence settled over these places of worship, and people traveled from all over the world to experience it. People did not come from all around the world because of a personality or a great sermon, but they came because of the glory of the Spirit of God being made manifest.

We even see this within the Bible when God manifested Himself in the midst of the ark to show the rest of the world that He was the God of Israel. He didn't manifest Himself anywhere else in the world! He manifested Himself only in the midst of Israel.

Even on the day of Pentecost, God made Himself known to 120 people who were praying for the promise that Jesus said would come. As these desperate, hungry ones waited with great anticipation, God manifested His glory through the power of

His Spirit and everyone knew it, to say the least! Even those who were not at the meeting still heard the sound when He broke into that little prayer meeting! (See Acts 2.) The thing I love about this story is that God doesn't need thousands or really even 120 people to do a mighty work. He only needs one burning heart who longs to taste His glory. This one thing right here is enough for Him to manifest His weighty presence. One hungry heart is the majority!

One of my favorite prophetic promises in the Bible concerning glory is found in Habakkuk.

> *For the earth will be filled with the knowledge of the glory of the Lord, as the waters cover the sea* (Habakkuk 2:14 NKJV).

As I meditated more closely on this prophetic promise, I realized that this was not just something God wanted, but it was actually the dream in His heart. The words *with the knowledge* in Hebrew are *yada*, which means to know by experience. The dream of God's heart is that the earth would not just know about His glory but would know His glory by experience! He wants you, me, and the rest of the world to know Him and experience His great glory! I believe in these last days God is looking for those who will pick up this prophetic promise found in Habakkuk and position themselves to do whatever it takes to see the dream of God's heart realized. He's not looking for experts; He's looking for burning hearts who have His dream in mind.

DISCERNING THE GLORY

In my quest to do my part in seeing the dream of God fulfilled, I began to look more closely at what the glory is and is not. I wanted to know how the glory manifests, how to recognize the glory and discover its different aspects. As I looked into the Bible as well as revival history, I discovered that the glory usually will manifest in two different ways with various vehicles of transportation. When I say vehicles of transportation, I mean modes in which He manifests Himself. Here are the two ways that I found.

1. Shekinah Glory

Although the word *Shekinah* is not technically in the Bible, we must still look at this term because it has been used throughout history in rabbinic literature as one way to describe God's glory. *Shekinah* comes from a Semitic root that means "to settle, inhabit, or dwell." According to Bible Study Tools, the Shekinah glory "is the visible manifestation of the presence of God. It is the majestic presence or manifestation of God in which He descends to dwell among men."[2] It's the invisible becoming visible. This is the glory being seen by the eye.

Here are a few examples of Shekinah glory or "glory that can be seen" that I found in the Bible, revival history, and of course my personal experiences. They would include but are not limited to fire, smoke, a burning bush, manna on the ground, creative miracles, gold dust, feathers, supernatural rain, resurrection of the dead, and supernatural oil manifesting. The Shekinah of God is an outward expression that He is present, which often manifests through signs, wonders, and miracles. I will explain in later chapters some of these manifestations and how God uses them to reveal His glory.

2. Kabod Glory

As mentioned earlier, one of the words for *glory* is *kabod,* which is defined as His weighty presence. I would like to suggest that this is the glory that is tangibly felt. Again, this would include but is not limited to being slain under the power of God or falling down because the weight of glory is so strong that you cannot stand. I would consider it to also be felt by people through holy laughter, trembling, shaking, or tears of love (weeping).

Again, I will take time in chapters ahead to describe some of these glory manifestations as well as testimonies of those who have experienced these vehicles of glory.

ANOINTING AND GLORY

In order for us to better understand the glory, we must know the difference between the anointing and the glory. The word *anointing* is used all throughout the Bible and was often used to place God's seal of approval, authorization, and consecration on kings, prophets, and priests. The synoptic gospels as well as some of the epistles also refer to the word *anointing*. Let's take a look at four New Testament passages to get a better understanding.

> *But you have an anointing from the Holy One, and you know all things* (1 John 2:20 NKJV).

> *The Spirit of the Lord is upon Me, because He has anointed Me to preach the gospel to the poor; He has sent Me to heal the brokenhearted, to proclaim liberty to the captives and recovery of sight to the blind, to set at liberty those who are oppressed; to proclaim the acceptable year of the Lord* (Luke 4:18-19 NKJV).

> *How God anointed Jesus of Nazareth with the Holy Spirit and with power, who went about doing good and healing all who were oppressed by the devil, for God was with Him* (Acts 10:38 NKJV).

You shall receive power when the Holy Spirit has come upon you (Acts 1:8 NKJV).

The word *anointed* in the Greek is *chrio,* which means to anoint, to consecrate, to furnish with the necessary powers for kingdom administration, to endue Christians with the gifts of the Holy Spirit, and to smear with oil to consecrate to an office or religious service. In other words, the anointing is God smearing us with a supernatural ability to fulfill our assignment to advance the Kingdom. It is God's consecration, authorization, and endowment to work the works of Christ on the earth.

The anointing of the Holy Spirit is so special to the believer. We need the anointing in order to be effective in life and in ministry or we are finished. We are all born with special gifts that are unique to our purpose and calling in life. But gifts without anointing will not accomplish anything. It's the anointing that destroys yokes of oppression, bondage, and demonic strongholds—not gifts! Miriam and I have always taught our children that people need more than your gifts; they need the anointing. My daughter Kathryn has an extraordinary gift from God as a songwriter and worship leader. We've always encouraged her, before ministering to others, to encounter Jesus privately first and let His precious anointing fall upon her—then go minister publicly. Every time she has done this, the minute she opens her mouth to sing it's as though the heavens are open and you feel the tangible presence of God in the room. It's absolutely incredible.

I've had the wonderful privilege to hear many great worship leaders and preachers who are quite gifted but unfortunately have no anointing. Again, people don't need our gifts; they need the precious anointing of the Holy Spirit operating in and on believers.

Lives depend on those who are saturated with the anointing oil of the Holy Spirit and fire.

The good news is that we have access through the blood of Jesus to an unlimited supply of anointing. The anointing is like God's holy perfume that carries divine power. The only way to get this precious anointing upon your life is through *secret place* intimacy with Jesus. For example, when my kids come sit on my lap and spend time with me, they walk away with the aroma of my cologne on them. I've heard my wife many times tell the kids, "You smell like Daddy." That's the anointing! When you and I spend time with Jesus, the perfume that He is wearing rubs off on us! As my kids leave my presence wearing my cologne on them, you and I both know that the smell of my cologne will only last for a day or so. They must come back daily in order for them to carry an ongoing aroma of their daddy. It's the same for the anointing. We must go back daily to receive fresh Holy Spirit anointing oil. It's the oil of intimacy on our lives that brings people, cities, and nations into revival. I will spend more time on this in the next chapter.

John Kilpatrick, who was the pastor during the Brownsville revival, says, "We work under the anointing but we rest under the glory."[3] I would agree. The anointing comes upon men and women to work the works of God in partnership with God. When men and women move in the glory realm, it's God at work. This is where you will see mass miracles and deliverances taking place without anyone laying hands on them. It's like when the apostle Peter would walk the streets of Jerusalem and people would bring the sick hoping that just the shadow of Peter would touch them so they'd receive healing (see Acts 5:15). It was not the shadow of Peter; it was the glory that rested on Peter that brought the miracles! I would like to suggest here that Peter was anointed to carry glory! He was set apart and smeared with the oil of the Holy Spirit to carry God's manifest presence everywhere he went.

FROM ANOINTING TO GLORY

Many of you are already moving in the anointing, and that is great news! Again, when we operate under the anointing, we are working as one authorized by God to work the works of Christ by the power of His Spirit. When God anoints someone, it gives them the endowment and authorization needed to prophesy, to heal the sick, to work miracles, to preach, to impart, to administrate, to bring forth deliverance, and to destroy yokes of oppression. In these last days, however, I believe God is pouring out an anointing to carry *the glory.* Instead of just moving in the anointing as people at work, many will begin to move in the glory in which heaven's activity is at hand upon the one who carries it and in whom God is at work. I believe God is releasing an anointing that will authorize people to carry His atmosphere in such a way that entire regions come under the influence of the Almighty. Those who carry this anointing will experience what I call *accidental miracles,* in which people get healed, set free, and delivered just by being in the same room.

Again, as referenced earlier, it's that same grace that was upon the apostle Peter. The Holy Spirit has revealed to me that this next move of God will be a revival of God's great glory, and He is anointing people now to prepare the earth for what He is about to do.

In her book *Revival Glory,* Ruth Ward Heflin says, "What God wants to do in these last days can only be accomplished in the glory realm."[4]

I would like to close this chapter by stating again that God is raising up and anointing those who will carry, stand in, release, impart, and minister in the glory realm of God. This great glory will usher in the greatest harvest of souls that the earth has ever seen. Get ready for the glory!

Let's pray:

> Thank You that You have chosen me to be a carrier of Your glory. Help me, Holy Spirit, to grow in my understanding of the glory through revelation and experience, in Jesus's name. Amen.

NOTES

1. Ruth Ward Heflin, *Glory* (Hagerstown, MD: McDougal Publishing, 1990), front matter.

2. Bible Study Tools, "The Abiding Presence of God," https://www.biblestudytools.com/commentaries/revelation/related-topics/the-abiding-presence-of-god.html.

3. John Kilpatrick, "Mysteries of the Glory," https://youtu.be/z3PWB_yp1HM?list=PLjY10K3dzUjplj6m1ct6i-wZNCpdybObaI&t=2166.

4. Ruth Ward Heflin, *Revival Glory* (Hagerstown, MD: McDougal Publishing, 1998), 92.

CHAPTER 3

FELLOWSHIP WITH THE SPIRIT OF GLORY

And I will pray the Father, and He will give you
another Helper, that He may abide with you forever.
—JOHN 14:16 NKJV

I want to take time in this chapter to talk to you about my dearest friend and Lord, the Holy Spirit. This chapter is probably the most special to my heart because I am writing about someone I love deeply and who means the world to me. I have come to know the Holy Spirit personally over the years, and I am still discovering even more about Him. You and I have the wonderful privilege, through the shed blood of Jesus, to get to know more fully this most precious person, the Holy Spirit. In fact, we get the rest of eternity to discover

the depths of who He is. Apart from Him we can do nothing, and this definitely includes moving in *the glory.*

R.A. Torrey says, "Before one can correctly understand the work of the Holy Spirit, he must first of all know the Spirit Himself."[1]

IDENTIFYING THE HOLY SPIRIT

The Bible teaches us that the Holy Spirit is one of three persons of the triune Godhead. God is one with three distinct personas in which He reveals Himself—Father, Son, and Holy Spirit. In other words, the Holy Trinity is co-equal and co-eternal, one in essence, nature, power, action, and will. They are one as it pertains to their divine nature but different in assignment. When describing the role of the Holy Spirit as it pertains to the Trinity, Judson Cornwall says,

> The Holy Spirit is a personality separate and distinct from God. He proceeds from God, is sent from God, and is God's Gift to people. Yet the Spirit is not independent of God. He always represents the one God. Just how the Holy Spirit can be one with God and yet distinct from God is part of the mystery of the Trinity.[2]

In his book *Good Morning, Holy Spirit,* Pastor Benny Hinn says that "the Trinity is the glory of God. God the Father is the glory of God; God the Son is the glory of God; and God the Holy Spirit is the glory of God. But who manifests that glory? It is the Holy Spirit. That is part of His work."[3]

The Bible calls the Holy Spirit eternal, which means He always has been and always will be (see Hebrews 9:14). He is the beginning and the end. The Holy Spirit is also known as the "Spirit of Christ" (see Romans 8:9; 1 Peter 1:11; Galatians 4:6).

He is omnipresent, which means He has the ability to be everywhere all at one time (see Psalm 139:7-10). In fact, I would like to suggest to you that God the Father and God the Son are in heaven, but God the Holy Spirit is the only one of the Godhead here on earth with us at this present moment. This is why we must pursue a relationship with Him! We cannot live without Him!

Remember what Jesus said in John 16:7 (NKJV): *"It is to your advantage that I go away; for if I do not go away, the Helper will not come to you; but if I depart, I will send Him to you."* Thanks be unto God that we don't have to live out this life alone! Without the Holy Spirit, we could never live out the Christian life that Jesus paid for.

The Holy Spirit is omnipotent, which means He is all powerful (see Luke 1:35). We see in the beginning of creation that the Holy Spirit was the one who was hovering over the earth releasing creative power to bring forth creation. The Holy Spirit is not *a* power; He is *the* power. He is the *dunamis* of heaven! That is why Jesus said in Acts 1:8 (NLT), *"you will receive power when the Holy Spirit comes upon you."* When the Holy Spirit comes upon a believer, that person now has the ability to be a bold witness, to preach the gospel, and to move in signs, wonders, and miracles. When the Holy Spirit touches the life of someone, because He is power, that power is now dispensed through that individual to bring forth glory in the earth. Every miracle, healing, sign, wonder, deliverance, or prophecy that we read in Scripture came through the Holy Spirit, who is power.

The Holy Spirit is omniscient, which means He is all knowing (see 1 Corinthians 2:10-11). He knows everything about you and me. He is the prophetic Spirit who sees all things and makes them known to us by telling us things to come (see John 16:13). Miriam and I have the wonderful privilege of sitting on the Apostolic Council of Prophetic Elders with Generals International. About 60 apostles and prophets from around the world come together to collaborate and hear what God is saying for the nations. It is the Holy Spirit who brings forth prophetic utterances for the nations. It is the Holy Spirit who is showing us things to come and how to prepare nations for what He intends to do.

Paul the apostle describes the Holy Spirit as the riches of glory, the treasure in earthen vessels, and the glory that we behold that transforms us into the image of Christ (see Ephesians 1:18; 2 Corinthians 4:7; 3:18).

Peter the apostle describes Him as the Spirit of glory resting upon us (see 1 Peter 4:14). The book of Acts describes Him as the fire in our spirit (see Acts 2). He is the gift promised by Jesus, whom the Father would send in His name, and is the river of living water who bubbles up within us (see John 14:15; 7:37).

The Holy Spirit is the one who makes Jesus real to us and makes Him known. He also has come to us to help us, encourage us, and testify to us about Jesus (see John 15:26-27). The word *testify* in the Greek means to bear witness or to give witness. In other words, the Holy Spirit living on the inside of us bears witness with our spirit that Jesus not only lives but is alive in us! He is the Spirit of the living Christ living unlimited on the inside of us! The very reason that you believe that Jesus is Lord and Savior is a direct result of the Holy Spirit making a witness in your spirit.

However, even though Scripture reveals truths concerning Him, we can still go through life just knowing about Him and not actually knowing Him personally.

For example, when Miriam and I got married, we made a covenant before heaven and earth to be committed to one another until death do us part. However, even though a covenant was made, I still needed to make a decision to get to know her personally. I made a decision to find out what she likes and doesn't like, her favorite foods, what makes her happy, and what grieves her heart. Over the years, I learned to know her even through her body language. How? Because I know her personally. It's exactly the same with the Holy Spirit.

Paul the apostle exhorted the church not to grieve or quench the Holy Spirit. Why? Because He is a person. To grieve the Holy Spirit is to hurt His heart. Bad attitudes, unrepented sin, unforgiveness, and offense can grieve the Holy Spirit. Just as we would need to clean up our mess with a spouse, friend, or family member if we hurt them, we would absolutely need to do the same with the Lord. Our relationship with the Holy Spirit is the most important relationship of all relationships. In addition, to quench the Holy Spirit is to stop His flow in your life. This could be extinguishing His fiery passion within us or simply not yielding to His leading.

Whether it is a relationship with your spouse, parent, child, friend, or the Lord, to know someone intimately will always take time. Great relationships come only through ongoing communion, and it is the same for knowing the Spirit. God forbid that Jesus die on the cross just so we can know about the Holy Spirit and not know Him personally.

I personally know what it's like to live life not knowing Him even though He has been with me since my salvation. Life not knowing Him is boring, dead, and lifeless. Life not knowing Him will only be ordinary with no adventure. The beauty of knowing the Holy Spirit is that through intimacy He can take your ordinary life and make it extraordinary! Knowing Him propels all of us into a life of joy, faith, adventure, miracles, power, and purpose. The Bible says that the Holy Spirit is our guide (see John 16:13). He not only guides us into all truth, but He guides us to promote us and propel us into our destiny!

Not too long ago, I owned part of my dad's irrigation business. One day, I began to dream of being used for revival and preaching the gospel all over the world. I started to have a deep desire to pursue the *more* of God. Little did I know that it was the Holy Spirit who was planting those dreams and desires in my heart. Through a series of events and confirmations, we left everything to move to Redding, California, to be a part of the Bethel movement and to learn from a family of revivalists who were changing the world. As we decided to follow the Holy Spirit's direction, we had no idea that our lives would be forever changed.

I would not be writing this book, nor would I even be where I am today, had it not been for that guidance of the Holy Spirit leading us to Redding for that particular season. We went from a boring, mundane life to traveling the world holding revival gatherings and miracle services, writing books, starting supernatural schools, and being on Christian television programs. Again, none of this would have been possible had it not been for the Holy Spirit. And I've got some really good news! The Holy Spirit will never guide you or me into a place where we will fail!

He only guides us into places of promotion, equipping, favor, and victory!

It is only by knowing Him that we can step into a world of true adventure experiencing His life, His work, His anointing, and of course His glory.

THE PERSONALITY OF THE HOLY SPIRIT

What makes up a person is not a physical body. Our physical bodies are the point of contact that gives our person a connection within the earth realm. Your person is your spirit man, who has a will, emotions, intellect, feelings, desires, and of course your personality. It is the same for the Holy Spirit. Remember, the Bible says that we are created in His image! (See Genesis 1:27.) As mentioned earlier, the Holy Spirit is a person too. When we receive Jesus, our physical body becomes a resting place in the earth for two persons to be joined together, becoming one. It is your person and the person of the Holy Spirit.

Paul the apostle made this clear in his address to the church in Corinthians when he said, *"But he who is joined to the Lord is one spirit with Him"* and *"do you not know that your body is the temple of the Holy Spirit?"* (1 Corinthians 6:17,19 NKJV).

We become one! We become Spirit to spirit, Person to person with the Lord! As we engage with Him in holy communion, we will begin to better know His person, His emotions, His intellect, His will, and of course His personality. As we commune with Him, a holy synergy takes place between us and the Spirit of God. As we behold Him, we become like Him. Wow! The God of the universe has made Himself available for us to get to know Him personally through holy union, Spirit to spirit!

We even have access to know what His personality is like. I believe that when Paul the apostle was referring to the fruits of the Spirit in Galatians, he was actually referring to the personality of the Holy Spirit. Let's take a look at what he was describing:

> But the fruit of the Spirit is love, joy, peace, longsuf-fering, kindness, goodness, faithfulness, gentleness, self-control (Galatians 5:22-23 NKJV).

I used to think that these fruits listed in Galatians 5 were a list of to-dos in order to walk in the Holy Spirit. However, now I have come to understand that these fruits are actually what make up the Holy Spirit's attributes and of course His personality. The fruit of His Spirit will never be produced in our lives by striving or performing, but it will only come by beholding His presence. As we behold Him, His personality begins to affect ours and we begin to manifest His life through ours.

MOVING INTO KNOWING HIM

The only way to truly know Him is through ongoing commu-nion—period, the end. There is no other way. And may I add, we will never move into realms of glory nor carry glory apart from knowing the Holy Spirit personally. Why? Because it all belongs to Him. It's His presence. His atmosphere. His glory.

Before I go any further, I want to say here that we must never pursue a relationship with the Holy Spirit just so we can carry His glory or receive some special anointing. We must never use the Holy Spirit! However, as you pursue an authentic relationship with this most precious gift, the result will always be His life invading yours. His power, His anointing,

His fruit, and His glory capturing your humanity and possessing your heart.

Everything that I currently possess has become a manifestation of what I have stewarded in a life of ongoing communion. I have learned and am still learning how to simply abide in Him through His indwelling presence. *"But the anointing which you have received from Him abides in you"* (1 John 2:27 NKJV). Once we receive Christ, we all have the same opportunity to learn to commune with Him and abide through the anointing of His indwelling presence. Thanks be to God for that!

In later chapters, I will talk more about His manifest presence, which is altogether different, but for now let's keep discussing the most important foundation—communion. This is where it all begins.

Paul the apostle, in his closing statement to the church in Corinth, said, *"The grace of the Lord Jesus Christ, and the love of God, and the* communion of the Holy Spirit *be with you all. Amen"* (2 Corinthians 13:14 NKJV). The word *communion* here in the Greek means to fellowship, to participate, and to be intimate with one another. The word for *intimate* means to be "close to" or intimate friends.

The great news is that we don't have to summon Him or strive to know Him. The Holy Spirit is already there waiting for us to turn toward Him and commune with Him. The Bible says that He will never leave us and will be with us forever (see John 14:15-17). Remember, because of the blood of Jesus we have become one with the Holy Spirit. If this be true, then the only thing we need to do is turn toward Him and talk with Him. You can even do that right now! Just turn your affections toward Him and tell

Him how much you love Him. The apostle James tells us, if we draw near to God, He will draw near to us (see James 4:8)!

I'm even feeling in my spirit right now as I write this book that the Holy Spirit is saying, "Do not downgrade your current connection with Me." In other words, do not minimize where you are right now with the Lord or your current connection with Him. Sure, we always can grow in relationship with the Holy Spirit, but don't you dare downgrade where you are right now with the Lord. Do not let condemnation, guilt, and shame come upon you just because you feel like you're not doing enough! That is a lie! God is so proud of where you are right now because it's not where you were! He just wants you to know that there is more and to keep exploring the depths of who He is. He's got more for you! He wants to know you more and for you to know Him!

I love how The Passion Translation presents this passage. Jesus was telling His disciples about the promised Holy Spirit: *"And I will ask the Father and he will give you another Savior, the Holy Spirit of Truth, who will be to you a friend just like me—and he will never leave you"* (John 14:16 TPT).

He not only wants us to know Him as Lord, but He also wants us to know Him as a friend! He wants us to know Him and hear His voice minute by minute and day by day. It is His deepest desire that you and I do life with Him. This has been His divine plan all along—intimate friends who co-labor together in life.

This was and still remains the secret power for every great revivalist in the Bible and in revival history. People like John and Carol Arnott, pastors of the Toronto outpouring, and Pastor Claudio Freidzon of the Argentine Revival understood this secret power. God not only sent these revivalists great, earth-shaking revivals, but they became carriers of glory themselves because they made a decision to wholeheartedly pursue a personal friendship with the Holy Spirit. Men and women of the faith all throughout history who moved heaven and earth did not just know God as God but as an intimate friend.

One of my favorite healing revivalists of all time was a woman by the name of Kathryn Kuhlman. Miss Kathryn Kuhlman wasn't the best preacher in the world, but when she took the stage it was as though all of heaven was in the room.

Kathryn was known for knowing the Holy Spirit. She once said, "There are literally thousands and thousands in the great charismatic movement who have never become acquainted with the person of the Holy Spirit, only with His gifts."[4]

Kathryn Kuhlman referred many times to the Holy Spirit as her best friend. She would often be found behind the stage right before one of her healing crusades just spending time with the Holy Spirit. Anywhere Kathryn would go, the Holy Spirit would go with her. The power of His presence attended her.

Why would the Holy Spirit manifest His glory in such profound ways in her meetings? I believe it was because the Holy Spirit trusted her. Trust is only earned through intimacy. I can always discern between ministers who have personal relationships with the Holy Spirit and those who do not. It is quite evident, to say the least. Think about it this way: when the Holy Spirit shares His glory with someone, it means that the Holy Spirit has given Himself to someone He trusts deeply. It's Him becoming vulnerable to an intimate friend. Miss Kuhlman, I believe, exemplified this.

Again, Pastor Benny Hinn shares a story in his book *Good Morning, Holy Spirit* about how the Holy Spirit attended Kathryn Kuhlman, manifesting His glory even in the most unusual places:

> In New York City, Kathryn Kuhlman had just finished preaching at a Full Gospel Business Men's convention. She was taken through the kitchen to an elevator to avoid the crowd. The cooks had no idea a meeting was going on and had never heard of Miss Kuhlman. In their white hats and aprons, the cooks didn't even know she was walking by, and the next thing you know they were flat on the floor. Why? Kathryn didn't pray for them; she just walked. What happened? When she left the meeting it seemed as though the power of His presence attended her.[5]

You might be asking, how and why does stuff like this happen? It happens because it is the power of His presence attending intimate friends wherever they go. People like Miss Kathryn Kuhlman give themselves to a life of fellowship with the Holy Spirit.

Fellowship with the Holy Spirit never has to be religious; it just needs to be real and authentic. Communion with God doesn't have to be somber and in a dark room somewhere with a bunch of clothes hanging on the wall and shoes on the floor. (Hence, prayer closet. Okay, I'm kidding.) I have made a decision to live from a *life* of prayer, not just a *time* of prayer. Prayer to me is simply communing with God spirit to Spirit throughout the day.

Talking with the Holy Spirit throughout the day is life-giving to me, as is setting aside special times of the day to get alone with God just to be still. Being still is leaning into God with expectation and simply waiting for the Lord. It may look like a walk, a drive, opening up the Bible and talking with Him about the Scriptures. It could be enjoying a cup of coffee with some worship music on, journaling the whispers of His voice, or praying in the Spirit.

As we make a decision to become intentional in communion with the Lord, we will learn to live from a place of unbroken fellowship with the Holy Spirit. And yes, all of this can even be in a prayer closet! Whatever works for you, as long as you are setting aside some time during your day to simply be still.

Now, I do want to add here that we must always be cautious not to reduce our relationship with the Holy Spirit down to a time slot of the day. If we do, we are missing a wonderful opportunity to learn to live a life of abiding in Him. Abiding in Him throughout the day must be the priority. It's not the length of our prayer time that moves God's heart but a life laid down in surrender that moves Him.

When Kathryn Kuhlman was asked about her prayer life, she replied,

> I pray all the time because if I limit the Holy Spirit to a certain number of hours a day, I would be in danger of using Him for my own purpose. If, for instance, I spent an hour a day in prayer, I would expect the Holy Spirit to reward me for that hour. I would begin to feel that it was that hour in prayer that caused the "anointing" in the meeting. No, I cannot use the Holy Spirit in that way. I must practice His presence all of the time.[6]

How to "practice His presence" will be discussed in the next chapter. You and I will never step into the greater glory or the fullness of our divine calling apart from learning to "practice His presence." Before one can move in the power and glory of the Holy Spirit, one must first know the Holy Spirit personally. And this, my friends, requires practice.

Let's pray:

> *Holy Spirit, I want Your fellowship. Will You take me deeper? Will You bring me into fellowship? Thank You, Lord, that You are the One who draws me by Your side. I love You. Amen.*

NOTES

1. R. A. Torrey, *The Person and Work of the Holy Spirit* (New York, NY: Fleming H. Revell, 1910), 1.

2. Judson Cornwall, *Releasing the Glory* (New Kensington, PA: Whitaker House, 2000), 40.

3. Benny Hinn, *Good Morning, Holy Spirit* (Nashville, TN: Thomas Nelson, 1997), 70.

4. Kathryn Kuhlman and Jamie Buckingham, *A Glimpse into Glory* (Alachua, FL: Bridge-Logos, 1983), 102.

5. Hinn, *Good Morning, Holy Spirit,* 52.

6. Jimmie McDonald, *The Kathryn Kuhlman I Knew* (Shippensburg, PA: Destiny Image Publishers, 1996).

CHAPTER 4

Practicing the Presence

Father, I desire that they also whom You gave
Me may be with Me where I am, that they may
behold My glory which You have given Me; for
You loved Me before the foundation of the world.
—John 17:24 NKJV

Over the years, I have had the wonderful privilege of being around others I would consider to be those who are anointed to carry glory, some of whom ended up becoming spiritual fathers of mine. It seems like just yesterday when Miriam and I moved to Redding to be a part of what God was doing at Bethel Church under the leadership of Pastor Bill Johnson. Once during a Friday night

service, Pastor Bill began to worship the Lord and just embrace His presence as a physical cloud of golden glory filled the room. This was not a vision or a figment of my imagination; it was a visible manifestation of God's glory. Everyone in the room saw it. We were all caught up in tears of joy and awe as we stood in the cloud of glory together. Jesus was glorified and people were blessed that night by this precious encounter. I realized then that we were with one whom I would consider a carrier of glory. Again, one who is anointed to carry glory is one who has been entrusted by the Holy Spirit to carry the manifest presence of God, whether or not it is seen or felt tangibly.

Miriam and I love the nations, and we absolutely love the nation of Brazil. We have been privileged to minister all over this beautiful nation together many times. During one of my missionary travels there, I met a man by the name of Dan Duke who is an obvious glory carrier. For those of you who have not heard of Dan, he is an American who was called many years ago to the nation of Brazil. God mightily used both Dan and his wife Marti, as the catalysts in the Brazilian revival of the 1990s. Often when Dan or Marti minister, the entire building is filled with the tangible presence of the Lord, and many people are blessed because of it. Since then, I have had the privilege of being considered a son by the Dukes, and for that I am eternally grateful.

Both the Dukes and Pastor Bill, as well as other great revivalists, have played an integral role in my growth of learning to practice the presence.

So you might be asking, "What exactly is practicing the presence of God?"

According to the *Oxford English Dictionary*, the word *practice* is a verb that means to carry out a particular activity habitually or regularly. Practicing the presence, I believe, is just that—connecting habitually and regularly with the manifest presence of God. You and I will never learn to carry the glory or walk in miracles or revival apart from learning to practice the presence.

As mentioned in the previous chapter, the foundation for practicing the presence is communion with the Holy Spirit. Neither I nor anyone else can practice the presence of God for you. You are the steward of your own journey. I can, however, give you some biblical insight as well as practical steps to creating space for you to grow in the art of practicing the presence. The Bible says,

> *To Him who loved us and washed us from our sins in His own blood, and has made us kings and priests to His God and Father, to Him be glory and dominion forever and ever. Amen* (Revelation 1:6 NKJV).

For the sake of discussion, I want to take a moment to focus on what I believe to be our highest priority as New Testament believers—our priestly role. The New Testament priesthood that we are called to must never be secondary but must remain primary in order for us to know what it is to practice the presence practically.

There are two things about our priestly assignment that we must know in order to learn how to practice the presence of the Lord. Knowing these two things gives us insight into positioning ourselves in preparation for the glory resting on us.

The first thing we need to understand is that only the priesthood carries the presence of the Lord. According to God's design, only the priests were set apart to carry the presence—the ark of the covenant (see Numbers 4:15; Deuteronomy 31:9).

When King David wanted to bring the ark of the presence (covenant) back to Jerusalem, he first made a grave mistake by putting the ark on a cart. As a result, a man by the name of Uzzah died. When the ox pulling the ark stumbled, he reached out to steady it on the cart. David went back to the drawing board and understood that the ark of the covenant was never meant to rest on a cart but only on the shoulders of the priesthood (see 2 Samuel 6:1-15). It's the same for us today. Only those whose hearts are postured as priests to the Lord will be the ones who will carry the manifest presence of God.

I believe wholeheartedly that the Old Covenant was a shadow of what was to come through the New Covenant found in Jesus Christ. With this being said, the Old Covenant reveals God's design for the priesthood to carry the manifest presence. The main job of the priesthood was to minister directly to the Lord and carry the ark of the covenant. We make a huge mistake by making our ministries all about *ministering to people*. The priority of ministry must never be people or the needs around us. The focus of our ministries must always be unto the Lord. From this place of ministering to the Lord, all other ministry flows. This is the heart posture of a New Testament priest.

The second thing that we need to understand about our priesthood is that as priests we are called to be keepers of the flame of God. It is the fire of God that prepares us for glory. The fire of God purifies and refines us, consecrating us to carry the manifest presence of God. The fire of His presence keeps our hearts tender and responsive before Him. It is the very thing that ignites a deep passion for Jesus and keeps us in pursuit of ongoing encounters with Him.

This holy fire was so important to God that He gave Moses further instructions concerning it:

> *And the fire on the altar shall be kept burning on it; it shall not be put out. And the priest shall burn wood on it every morning, and lay the burnt offering in order on it; and he shall burn on it the fat of the peace offerings. A fire shall always be burning on the altar; it shall never go out* (Leviticus 6:12-13).

If you study this passage, you will see that it was God who sent this supernatural fire, but it was the priests who had been commanded to keep it burning. This, to me, is a perfect example of co-laboring with God for revival glory. God is always faithful to send His fire, His glory, and revival for that matter, but we must learn to steward it well by keeping it going.

The apostle Paul, in his letter to the church in Thessalonica, exhorted these believers to make sure to not "put out" the fire of the Holy Spirit (see 1 Thessalonians 5:19). Practicing the presence is what we do to keep the fire of God burning in our heart.

Again, to practice something is to carry out an activity habitually or regularly.

TWO KEYS THAT WILL POSITION YOUR HEART TO PRACTICE THE PRESENCE

1. Decide to Die Daily

> [Jesus said,] *"If anyone desires to come after Me, let him deny himself, and take up his cross daily, and follow Me. For whoever desires to save his life will lose it, but*

whoever loses his life for My sake will save it" (Luke 9:23-24 NKJV).

[The apostle Paul said,] *"I affirm, by the boasting in you which I have in Christ Jesus our Lord, I die daily"* (1 Corinthians 15:31 NKJV).

This is a daily decision. We as people of God must learn to harness the power of decision. Every decision that we make will *manifest a result,* whether it be good or bad. There are decisions we can make today that will either positively or negatively affect our lives. The priests in Leviticus had to make a decision to obey God and to keep the fire of God burning daily (see Leviticus 6:12-13). The fire on the altar required daily attendance. It is the absolute same in practicing the presence of the Lord through ongoing fellowship. Any deep relationship will always come at a cost. I believe it is time to "buy oil," according to the parable of the ten virgins that Jesus talked about in Matthew 25:

> *Then the kingdom of heaven shall be likened to ten virgins who took their lamps and went out to meet the bridegroom. Now five of them were wise, and five were foolish. Those who were foolish took their lamps and took no oil with them, but the wise took oil in their vessels with their lamps. But while the bridegroom was delayed, they all slumbered and slept.*
>
> *And at midnight a cry was heard: "Behold, the bridegroom is coming; go out to meet him!" Then all those virgins arose and trimmed their lamps. And the foolish said to the wise, "Give us some of your oil, for our lamps are going out." But the wise answered, saying, "No, lest there should not be enough for us and you; but go rather*

to those who sell, and buy for yourselves" (Matthew 25:1-9 NKJV).

The gospel is absolutely free, but maturity will cost you everything. We will never carry the manifest presence of God in our lives by only living a "Sunday morning church service relationship" with Jesus. In other words, those who reduce their Christian life to Sunday mornings instead of living a life laid down daily will miss out on the life that Jesus paid for. Dying daily looks like you rearranging your schedule to be with Him. It looks like getting up an hour early so you can be intentional about being still and hearing His voice. Dying daily looks like living unoffended and forgiving quickly when others betray you. It looks like being fully yielded to Him and obeying no matter what the cost might be. A life laid down for the Lord will produce within us the "oil of intimacy," which will produce eternal fruit that remains. When you and I decide to die daily, we make room for the life and power of God to enter in. When we decide to lose our life for His sake, it is then that we truly find it!

Kathryn Kuhlman understood what it meant to die to herself:

> If you think it's easy to go to the cross, it's simply because you've never been there. I've been there. I know. And I had to go alone. I knew nothing of the power of the mighty third person of the Trinity which was available to all. I just knew it was four o'clock on Saturday afternoon and I had come to the place in my life where I was ready to give up everything—even Mister—and die. I said it out loud, "Dear Jesus, I surrender all. I give it all to you. Take my body. Take my heart. All I am is yours. I place it in your wonderful

hands." In that moment, I yielded to God in body, soul, and spirit. I gave him everything…. That afternoon, Kathryn Kuhlman died. And when I died, God came in, the Holy Spirit came in. There, for the first time, I realized what it meant to have power.[1]

Deciding to die daily looks like making a decision to prioritize connecting with the Holy Spirit every single day. It looks like setting aside time just to be with Him. It's time to put down the distractions and just be with the One who is worthy of our affection.

I love what God told John and Carol Arnott, pastors of the Toronto Outpouring, as they sought the "more" of God:

As we cried out to the Lord that night, He answered us. He said, "If you're serious, I'll give you two things to do. Number one, I want your mornings. And number two, I want you to hang around people who are anointed."[2]

Let's just decide right now that we are going to give God our mornings! After all, He is altogether worth it!

2. Decide to Drink Deeply through Praise and Worship

On the last day, that great day of the feast, Jesus stood and cried out, saying, "If anyone thirsts, let him come to Me and drink. He who believes in Me as the Scripture has said, out of his heart will flow rivers of living water" (John 7:37-38 NKJV).

We must learn to be heavy drinkers if we are going to carry glory. Jesus has made His water well available, but we must come to Him and drink deeply through praise and worship. It is high time to draw near to the Lord! As we draw near to Him, it's then that He draws nearer to us (see James 4:8). Be intentional today and draw near to Him. He's waiting for you! As you do this, He will fill you up to overflowing!

When writing to a church who had already experienced a measure of revival, Paul the apostle said, *"Therefore do not be unwise, but understand what the will of the Lord is. And do not be drunk with wine* [intoxicated, under the influence]...*but be filled with the Spirit"* (Ephesians 5:17-18 NKJV).

The will of God for you and me is to be continuously filled with the Holy Spirit. To be absolutely immersed, filled, and flooded with the manifest presence of the living God. You know you are full when you live a life of overflow. This, to me, is a sign that you are drinking deeply. The good news is that the Bible is clear that we have all been privileged to drink from the same Holy Spirit (see 1 Corinthians 12:13). Let's get to drinking!

PRAISE AND WORSHIP

As we decide to praise and worship daily, a supernatural power is released and an atmosphere conducive for drinking occurs. Praise in itself carries an ability to shift atmospheres and gets us on the same page with who God is. Let's take a look at what God does through praise:

- The Bible says that God inhabits the praises of His people (see Psalm 22:3). In other words, God invades our praise!

- Praise is a weapon that dismantles demonic strongholds, displaces heaviness, and silences our enemies!

Through the praise of children and infants you have established a stronghold against your enemies, to silence the foe and the avenger (Psalm 8:2 NIV).

- The prophet Isaiah released a prophetic decree in regard to the power of praise:

To console those who mourn in Zion, to give them beauty for ashes, the oil of joy for mourning, the garment of praise for the spirit of heaviness; that they may be called trees of righteousness, the planting of the Lord, that He may be glorified (Isaiah 61:3 NKJV).

- Praise is a battle strategy that prophesies the victory of the Lord!

Now after the death of Joshua it came to pass that the children of Israel asked the Lord, saying, "Who shall be first to go up for us against the Canaanites to fight against them?" And the Lord said, "Judah shall go up. Indeed I have delivered the land into his hand" (Judges 1:1-2 NKJV).

In her book *Glory,* Ruth Ward Heflin says we must "Praise until the Spirit of worship comes. Worship until the glory comes. Then stand in the glory."[3]

Praise looks like something. It is not a quiet, introverted soaking session. Now, I'm all for soaking in the Spirit, but soaking is not praise. When I praise, I choose to *will* myself to praise. I will offer my body, my lips, my soul to praise Jesus. Our praise becomes the sacrifice on the altar. It is the wood that keeps the fire burning. Now, I can will myself to praise, but I cannot will myself to worship. I praise until the spirit of worship falls upon me. As we praise the Lord, He begins to inhabit our praises, and we become utterly aware that He is in the room.

When the Spirit of Lord begins to manifest in the room, you will not be able to help but worship. You have now entered into the realm of glory. The realm of His manifest presence. Remember, this is the realm where creative miracles flow. This the realm of divine revelation and encounter. This is the realm of drinking from the well.

Let me give you an example that Ruth Ward Heflin uses to explain what happens when praise leads to worship, which results in glory being manifested.

Let's say that you heard that Jesus was in your city and He was going to walk down a certain street at a certain time. You go stand there and wait for Him to walk by. As you stand there on the street waiting, you begin to hear loud praises erupt all around you, and you decide to join this orchestra of praise. You and others are there crying out, "Holy, holy, holy is the Lord God Almighty," as Jesus approaches. Then suddenly, Jesus stops in front of you and tells you and only you, "I love you."

I am sure that we all know what would happen next. You would not be able to help yourself. You would do the same thing anyone would do, I'm sure. Any one of us would fall on our faces in deep worship. Why? Because the Master is there, and it's just you and Him.

My friend, this is the place that I am talking about. This is the place of His manifest presence resting upon you. Deep worship is the place where His glory will be found. And it's this place where His fragrant oil rubs off on you. It's what we live for. Just to be found by Him. This is the place where we learn to abide. This is the place where the fire of His Spirit burns deep within us. This is the place of deep drinking.

It is high time to make room in our lives to turn on the worship music and just burn before Him. It is time to just turn our affections toward Him and let His love penetrate our hearts. This is the place in God that we were designed for. Deep worship is the place of "beholding as in a mirror the glory of the Lord."

The Lord waits daily for you. If we are going to be entrusted to carry His manifest presence, then we must be found by Him. We must make a decision to make room daily to be alone with Him. I don't want to go through a day without connecting with Him. I believe that we can live our lives in such a way that we live from a place of praise and deep worship. This place of deep worship is the heart posture that ministers directly to the Lord. Through the Holy Spirit, we have become true New Testament priests unto the Lord, who carry His manifest presence. Remember, it's only the priesthood that has been given the charge to carry His glory.

Again, we must never use or prostitute the Holy Spirit just so we can have a great meeting or some anointing. Rather, as we approach Him in spirit and truth, the fruit of that will always be glory.

As I mentioned earlier, I have learned a lot from spiritual fathers and mothers over the years. I have learned this specific aspect of daily worship from Dan Duke. Not only does he live a life of worship, but he chooses to practice this worship lifestyle among sons and daughters so that a generation will catch the wind. I'll never forget one time when Dan invited me and two other brothers to his room right before he was about to minister to about five thousand people in Belo Horizonte, Brazil. As we came into Dan's room, he turned on the worship music and we all sat on the floor and just burned together as we worshiped Jesus. It was incredible! Later, of course, the inevitable happened.

As Dan took the stage to minister, all of heaven came upon the entire auditorium. Why did the glory manifest so heavily in that meeting? It was because of a man who knew how to drink deeply by living a lifestyle of worship. It was because of a man who knew how to position himself as a priest unto the Lord. This is how we learn to "practice the presence." It's from a place of worship that we learn what carrying His presence is all about.

Let's pray:

> *Lord, I live for Your presence. Teach me, Holy Spirit, how to practice Your presence every day. Teach me how to know and discern Your precious presence in Jesus's name. Amen.*

NOTES

1. Kathryn Kuhlman, qtd. in Bill Johnson and Jennifer Miskov, *Defining Moments: Kathryn Kuhlman* (New Kensington, PA: Whitaker House, 2016), 237.

2. John and Carol Arnott, *Preparing for the Glory* (Shippensburg, PA: Destiny Image Publishers, 2018).

3. Ruth Ward Heflin, *Glory: Experiencing the Atmosphere of Heaven* (Hagerstown, MD: McDougal Publishing Company, 1990).

CHAPTER 5

FUEL FOR THE FIRE

Where there is no wood, the fire goes out.
—PROVERBS 26:20 NKJV

I heard Bill Johnson once say, "Come to me twenty years from now and take me out for coffee and tell me you're still burning for the more of God." His invitation provoked within me a deep longing in my heart to burn with holy passion for Jesus all the days of my life. It is so unfortunate that I have seen so many people burn with a passionate pursuit of Jesus right after salvation and later in life they turn cold as ice.

God will send His holy fire upon us, but you and I are responsible to keep that fire burning in our lives. We must give God something to burn or our lives will become lukewarm, apathetic, powerless, and indifferent.

The church at large must get back to the basics of the early church if we are going to see the greater works that Jesus promised (see John 14:12). If we want the power of the early church, then we must be willing to pay the price that they paid through prayer and living out the truths laid out in Scripture. God has given us everything that we need for life and godliness as well as moving in ongoing revival glory.

As we learn to *practice the presence,* there are three principles found in Scripture that can help us keep the fire burning as well as activate the supernatural power of God in our lives. When I started practicing these three things, the fire of God was ignited in me and I began to see greater measures of glory, miracles, and breakthroughs. Practicing these three things daily not only gave me access to greater realms of glory, but they also served as weapons in my hands that dismantled and displaced powers of darkness for me as well as for others I ministered to.

The world is counting on the fire of God burning bright within the hearts of His people. There is a lost and dying world that does not need powerless, apathetic Christians who carry no fire. Christians without fire are like meat without salt—bland and undesirable. The world is longing for a church on fire that burns with a passionate devotion for Jesus. It's a church on fire that gets the attention of the world. Let's make a decision together to keep the fire of God's presence burning in our hearts.

THREE THINGS TO KEEP THE FIRE BURNING

1. Press into Tongues (Praying in the Spirit)

> *And these signs will follow those who believe: In My name they will cast out demons; they will speak with*

new tongues; they will take up serpents; and if they drink anything deadly, it will by no means hurt them; they will lay hands on the sick, and they will recover (Mark 16:17-18 NKJV).

Paul the apostle believed in the power of praying in tongues. He wrote more epistles in the New Testament than any other apostle; God performed extraordinary miracles through him; and he had heavenly encounters, seeing things that he could not even talk about. While addressing the church in Corinth about the use of tongues, he said, *"I thank my God I speak with tongues more than you all"* (1 Corinthians 14:18 NKJV).

I think if the apostle Paul believed in the power of praying in tongues, then so must we. Unfortunately, tongues are probably one of the most underutilized and misunderstood secret weapons that God has given the body of Christ. The enemy of our soul tries his best to discredit the power of praying in the Spirit because it is extremely powerful for the believer.

Praying in tongues is the bridge that God uses to connect us to a life of signs, wonders, and miracle power. If we are going to access greater dimensions of His power and presence, then we must press into practicing daily prayer in the Spirit.

Understanding the Diversity of Tongues

And God has appointed these in the church: first apostles, second prophets, third teachers, after that miracles, then gifts of healings, helps, administrations, varieties [diversities] of tongues (1 Corinthians 12:28 NKJV).

The word *diversities* simply means differences. So this tells us that there are different supernatural flows or manifestations of tongues. For the sake of understanding, there are four types of tongues according to Scripture. The first three are absolutely sovereign, and it is God who wills them. They are tongues as a sign to the unbeliever, tongues for interpretation, and tongues of deep groaning (see 1 Corinthians 14:5,22; Acts 2; Romans 8:26).

The last type of tongues is the one I'm really referring to in this section. This type of tongue is for personal edification, and it requires a partnership with the Holy Spirit by our own initiative (see 1 Corinthians 14:4). We can use this supernatural language hour after hour as we desire. This type of tongue accompanies the baptism of the Holy Spirit. As we are immersed in the Holy Spirit, it is then that we are equipped with this supernatural prayer language. As we partner with God by opening up our mouths, letting this supernatural language flow, unlimited power is released and the fire of God within us is ignited at a whole new level.

Accessing Mountain-Moving Faith

He who speaks in an unknown tongue edifies himself (1 Corinthians 14:4 MEV).

But you, beloved, building yourselves up on your most holy faith, praying in the Holy Spirit, keep yourselves in the love of God (Jude 20-21 NKJV).

The word *edify* in the Greek means to build a house or to erect a building. When we pray in the Spirit, a supernatural building is being erected within us to contain the anointing of the Holy Spirit. In other words, if you want to grow in the anointing, pray in tongues often! As we pray in the Spirit, our capacity enlarges for a greater measure of glory to be manifested. Miracle power—authority to cast out demons and move big mountains—comes as a result of praying in the Spirit. Praying in the Spirit is the access point to receiving and connecting to the anointing of the Holy Spirit.

Again, when we pray in the Spirit, a superstructure is being built to make room for greater measures of anointing. I have made it a habit to pray in tongues all throughout the day. Doing this has launched me into new levels of glory and revelation that I never even knew existed. Oftentimes, we think that praying in the Spirit has to be loud and demonstrative to be effective. I would like to suggest that is simply not true. I pray quietly under my breath throughout the day, knowing that it is getting the job done.

The apostle Paul exhorted the church to pray without ceasing, but unfortunately much of the church has ceased to pray. I believe that praying in tongues is a way for you and me to engage in prayer throughout the day, connecting with the Spirit of God.

The Bible says, *"The effective, fervent prayer of a righteous man avails much"* (James 5:16 NKJV). I believe that praying in the Spirit continuously is what makes our prayers effective. Miracles are being unlocked and mountains are moving as we pray in the Spirit. I noticed several years ago when I started to pastor that engaging the church in corporate prayer (praying in the Spirit together) released great glory and manifested miracles among us. I believe this is one of the secrets to walking in power and revival glory.

Another thing I want to bring to your attention is that when we pray in this type of tongue, the Holy Spirit intercedes for us according to God's plan and is making intercession for our calling. Isn't that amazing! When we partner with Him by opening up our mouths and praying in tongues, the God of the universe prays His perfect will for us! (See Romans 8:27.) Not only for you, but your family and friends as well!

Stepping into the Spirit Realm of Revelation

While having a heavenly encounter, the apostle John said,

> *I was in the Spirit on the Lord's Day, and I heard behind me a loud voice, as of a trumpet, saying, "I am the Alpha and the Omega, the First and the Last," and, "What you see, write in a book and send it to the seven churches which are in Asia"* (Revelation 1:10-11 NKJV).

The early church fathers understood the power of praying in tongues. I believe that the apostle John stepped into the Spirit realm as he engaged in his heavenly prayer language. Every time you and I decide to pray in tongues, it activates and opens up the Spirit realm of revelation to us. If we want to grow in revelation, we must pray often in the Spirit!

The Bible says that the Holy Spirit within us searches for the deep things of God and makes them known to us (see 1 Corinthians 2:10). We need to understand the deep things of God if we are going to access greater realms of glory and divine wisdom for this hour. Even in the day-to-day, God will download specific wisdom and instruction that may be needed for the hour at hand. As we pray in tongues, we are actually speaking the wisdom of God in a mystery even though we don't understand it at the time. As we speak forth this precious wisdom in mystery first, the Holy Spirit draws it out and makes it known to our minds so that we can take action according to God's divine plan (see 1 Corinthians 2:7). This revelatory wisdom may come to you immediately, or it could come later at just the right time. I make it a daily habit to pray in the Spirit throughout the day. I always do this as I minister, because often I'm not sure what direction to take. As I engage my spirit in prayer, the Lord always comes with revelation and manifests His presence.

Let's pray in the Holy Spirit to add some fuel to the fire!

2. Press into the Word by "Decreeing a Thing"

> *Yahweh's Word is perfect in every way; how it revives our souls! Yahweh's laws lead us to truth, and his ways change the simple into wise. Yahweh's teachings are right and make us joyful; his precepts are so pure!* (Psalm 19:7-8 TPT)

I want to share a quick passage from our book *Decrees that Unlock Heaven's Power* on the power of the Word of God in us:

> You have been given a weapon. You have been given a promise book. You have been given a playbook that brings judgment on your enemies and a victory song to your heart. You have been given the Word of God. God's Word is not just a book of meaningless words on a page, but a book of power that carries weight. God's Word truly revives us and calibrates us to hear God's voice. It awakens us to destiny and presses us into purpose.[1]

Wow! There must be power in decreeing God's Word!

> *You will also declare a thing, and it will be established for you; so light will shine on your ways* (Job 22:28 NKJV).

> *There has not failed one word of all His good promise* (1 Kings 8:56 NKJV).

The late great healing evangelist Tommy Osborn said, "Any promise of God, when spoken, believed in, and acted upon is transformed into the power of God." In other words, making bold, faith-filled decrees leads to believing, and believing leads to action, which dispenses the power of God into given situations. Think about it—God created the universe with His own words!

While attending Bible school, Miriam and I were really struggling financially. Not only were we struggling to pay bills, but we felt like we were not walking in the fullness of God's plan for our lives. We saw others around us moving in their calling and changing the world, but not us. To be quite honest, even though we were in a really great church community and a great school, we were discouraged. It felt as if something wasn't connecting and we were misaligned.

We began to discover that there was a disconnect between our thinking and words and all that God had promised in the Bible. We felt a strong impression from the Lord that it was time for us to get on the same page with heaven. But how?

I heard one of the most profound statements from a man by the name of Zig Ziglar, who said, "You are what you are and where you are because of what has gone into your mind. You can change what you are and where you are by changing what goes into your mind."[2]

As he thinks in his heart, so is he (Proverbs 23:7 NKJV).

What?! You mean my thinking has everything to do with whether I enter into God's promises or not? The answer to my questions was a big fat *yes!*

Bill Johnson says, "Most closed heavens are between the ears." We began to realize that in order for us to see God's divine plan in our life and heaven's power unlocked, we needed a divine over-haul in our thinking. We needed to be transformed in our minds.

> *Be transformed by the renewing of your mind, that you may prove what is that good and acceptable and perfect will of God* (Romans 12:2 NKJV).

Miriam and I discovered that we can start transforming our minds by bringing transformation to the way we talk. This idea was reinforced when I went to Bible class one morning and I heard one of my professors challenge us to take twenty or so Bible verses and decree them out loud for the next forty days.

So we began to decree out loud God's promises over our marriage, our children, our destiny, our present, and our future. It was not long before we began to see a major breakthrough! As we began to make decrees, the power of God was unlocked and our lives began to change in a mighty way. It was like God put us on a path of acceleration.

God has given us a powerful tool. And that tool is His Word in our mouth! The Bible says, *"Death and life are in the power of the tongue"* (Proverbs 18:21 NKJV). Once Miriam and I began to understand this, we made it a priority to daily decree God's Word. We began to see miracles, revival, and doors of destiny open wide for us. Jesus said, *"If you abide in Me, and My* words abide in you, *you will ask what you desire, and it shall be done for you"* (John 15:7). It is the abiding word in us that gets supernatural answers!

As you and I press into the Word of God by leveraging the power of decrees, unlimited resources are made available to us. We become revived, filled, and flooded with all of God's good promises. God's Word becomes a fire shut up in our bones that propels us forward into the greater things.

3. Press into the Power of the Testimony

> *Take, for example, the sons of Ephraim. Though they were all equipped warriors, each with weapons, when the battle began they retreated and ran away in fear. They did not keep God's covenant and refused to live by his law. They forgot his wonderful works and the miracles of the past* (Psalm 78:9-11 TPT).

What?! These people were equipped warriors, but they turned back on the day of battle and ran with their tails between their legs! What happened? They forgot the testimony.

The Hebrew word for *testimony* actually comes from a root that means to "do again." There is power in keeping the testimony of Jesus hidden within your heart. The testimony was so important to God that He even commanded Israel to keep it close at all times.

> *Only be careful, and watch yourselves closely so that you do not forget the things your eyes have seen or let them fade from your heart as long as you live. Teach them to your children and to their children after them* (Deuteronomy 4:9 NIV).

Unfortunately, there were times in Israel's history when they forgot the testimony of the Lord. This led to generations arising that did not know the Lord or His works, resulting in decline (see the book of Judges). Thankfully, God always has a *plan B,* and that plan always includes someone who has hidden His Word deep within their heart. It is those who are immersed in His precious Word whom He uses to bring revival to cities and nations. Those who have not forgotten the testimony of the Lord. God always looks for someone who is willing to take up the testimony as a prophetic promise and stand in the gap until God does again what He has done before and even greater. The testimony of the Lord prophesies His intention for future generations.

The Power of the Testimony in Revival History

Historically, we see God using the testimony as fuel to spark revival in different places throughout the earth. For example, when God poured out His Spirit in Wales through Evan Roberts in 1904, someone by the name of Frank Bartleman heard what God was doing in Wales and began to believe God for the same in California. As Frank rallied others in prayer, God raised up William Seymour as the catalyst for what we now know as the Azusa Street Revival. Because people in California heard the testimony of what God was doing in Wales, it became the fuel that sparked revival in California in 1906. Pentecostalism spread throughout America because someone heard what was possible. The very same thing happened in India. People from India heard what God was doing in Wales, and it launched India into full-blown revival in 1905.

The same happened in the '90s. An incredible revival broke out in Argentina in 1992. People from Toronto heard about what God was doing in Argentina and began to cry out for a move of God in their region. This sparked another great revival in 1994 known as the Toronto Blessing. Again, people in Florida heard about what God was doing in Toronto and became hungry for the same. Their cries were heard in 1995, which resulted in the Brownsville Revival.

Just thinking about these great moves of God causes my heart to burn. I believe that we are again standing at the threshold of the appointed time in our history. God intends to do again what He has done before. Just as it was time for revival in the early 1900s and 1990s, it is time for revival again. God is looking now for those who will pick up the testimonies of the past as prophetic decrees and believe God until He pours it out.

The Bible says, *"The testimony of Jesus is the spirit of prophecy"* (Revelation 19:10 NKJV). In other words, when we hear or read a testimony of any kind, that testimony becomes a prophetic promise to us of God's intentions. I live for feasting on the testimony of others both in the present and in the past. When I do this, my faith is strengthened and my fire becomes ignited to reach out and take hold of God's promises by faith. I love to read revival history. I noticed many years ago when I started to learn about others and their God moments that it opened up a whole new world of encounter to me. I took those stories and testimonies as prophetic decrees to me. As I heard about others moving in miracles, glory, and revival, it sparked something within my heart that positioned me to receive the same.

I even remember when Miriam and I had our very first miracle service. At that time, we had not seen miracles through our own lives. We had only seen them through the lives of others. As we launched out in faith to conduct our first miracle service, we decided to share testimonies of what God had done through others. As we shared about the miracle power of Jesus, people started to line up to tell us that they had been supernaturally healed! To be honest, we were a little surprised. We could not believe what was happening. Dozens and dozens of people were healed that night in our very first miracle service all because we shared testimonies of what we had heard!

KEEPING IT PRACTICAL

Since then, we have experienced thousands of notable miracles and healings around the world. Why? Because Miriam and I have made a decision to feast on the testimony of Jesus. The culture even within our own home has become a place where the focus of our lives is about what God has done and is doing. Many nights our family will sit around the dinner table talking about what we have seen Jesus do. Often as a family, we will watch YouTube videos of miracle testimonies that are happening around the world just to keep the fire in our hearts burning for impossible situations to bow to Jesus.

As we talk about the testimony, it opens up realms of miracles, glory, revival, and encounter that propel us forward into the divine plan of God. Keeping the testimony hidden in our hearts throws fuel on the fire within us. Do whatever you can do today to keep the testimony of Jesus before you. Get books and watch videos of revivalists who moved in miracles and glory. By doing this, your heart will be ignited and your life will be changed.

Let's pray:

Holy Spirit, You are the fire in my spirit. You are the passion within my heart. Lord, help me to be diligent by throwing fuel on the fire of my heart every day. Amen.

NOTES

1. Tommy and Miriam Evans, *Decrees that Unlock Heaven's Power* (Shippensburg, PA: Destiny Image Publishers, 2021), 76-77.

2. Zig Ziglar, "Change What Goes into Your Mind," https://www
.ziglar.com/quotes/you-are-what-you-are-and-where-you-are.

CHAPTER 6

Accessing Glory

*And the glory which You gave Me I have given
them, that they may be one just as We are one.*
—John 17:22 NKJV

The great news is that you and I have unlimited access to God's glory. Jesus is the only way to this precious glory. There is no other way. Because of the shed blood of Jesus, we can approach the throne of grace with boldness as inheritors of His manifest presence.

Bill Johnson says, "The gospel is free, but maturity is expensive." I would agree with this statement. Though the resources of the Kingdom are free for the believer, they require a maturity of discovery to access them. As we mature in the Spirit, our weight-bearing capacity grows with it. It is our weight-bearing capacity that enables us

to carry the weightiness of His manifest presence that is needed most in these last days.

As I was in prayer earlier this year, the Lord began to download five things that will position us to access God's unlimited glory as well as multiply the anointing to carry more.

FIVE THINGS TO POSITION US TO ACCESS A MULTIPLIED ANOINTING FOR GLORY

1. Ask Big

Jesus said, *"Ask, and it will be given to you; seek, and you will find; knock, and it will be opened to you"* (Matthew 7:7 NKJV). The mighty Trinity wants us to ask big! Much of what we do not have is simply because we are not asking God for it. I'm not talking about asking for expensive cars and mansions. Of course, God owns everything, and He is willing to give us things that we need as well as bless us—that is for sure. But I'm talking about the incredible treasures of the Kingdom of God. The Lord has given us a divine invitation to ask and receive. I love it when my kids come to me and ask for things that they really want. As a good father, it is my pleasure to give to them and bless them. It is absolutely the same with our heavenly Father. He loves it when you and I come to Him in eager expectation, knowing that He will answer our prayers. It is the divine exchange of ongoing fellowship.

Anytime I have asked for a greater measure of anointing or to grow in the miraculous, the Lord always responds to my heartfelt requests with a big fat *yes!* It was when Miriam and I started to ask big that we began to receive. We started asking to be used in revival, and now we travel all over the world holding revival gatherings. We started asking God for a demonstration of His power to be present when we preached, and we began to see notable miracles in our meetings because of it. Why? Because we asked for it!

> *Ask of Me, and I will give You the nations for Your inheritance, and the ends of the earth for Your possession* (Psalm 2:8 NKJV).

It's time to ask for the nations! It's time to ask for the greater works to begin to be made manifest in and through our lives.

The early church understood the power of asking. Not only did they get what they were asking for on the day of Pentecost, but they even got upgraded to new levels as they continued to ask for more. The disciples had just received the baptism of the Holy Spirit, and they immediately began to preach the gospel with signs following. The passion and power they carried got the attention of their critics. Healing a man who had been crippled since birth led to them being imprisoned. After their release from prison, they were given strict orders to not preach in Jesus's name ever again. Instead of listening to those religious hecklers, they went straight to a prayer meeting! Their bold requests penetrated heaven and released another level of Holy Spirit power!

> *"Now, Lord, look on their threats, and grant to Your servants that with all boldness they may speak Your word, by stretching out Your hand to heal, and that signs and wonders may be done through the name of Your holy Servant Jesus." And when they had prayed, the place where they were assembled together was shaken; and they were all filled with the Holy Spirit, and they spoke the word of God with boldness* (Acts 4:29-31 NKJV).

These burning ones who had already received the baptism of the Holy Spirit, and who were already walking in a measure of glory, asked for more! They got what they were asking for! They got double! This must be our standard. You and I have permission to ask God for more! The biblical standard is more power, more glory, and fresh immersion of the Holy Spirit!

When addressing the church in Ephesus, Paul the apostle said,

Now to Him who is able to do exceedingly abundantly above all that we ask or think, according to the power that works in us, to Him be glory in the church by Christ Jesus to all generations, forever and ever. Amen (Ephesians 3:20-21 NKJV).

I love what Prophet Bobby Connors says: "You have permission to exaggerate God's goodness."

When we ask God for big things, He is already releasing exceeding and abundant big answer to our prayers! Our job is to ask. His job is to exceed it! If we want to see revival hit the planet again, we have got to ask for it. If we want to see miracles manifest through our lives and God's glory covering the earth, we've got to ask for it! When we ask for big things, our asking becomes an open door between heaven and earth that invites the King of Glory to come in.

Ask the Lord for rain in the time of the latter rain (Zechariah 10:1 NKJV).

It has been raining for over two thousand years, and it is time to ask again for the rain of outpouring. It is time to ask God for the more that He has promised for our families, our cities, and our nations.

If you want to be used in this hour to revive cities and nations, *ask*. If you want to move in the power of the Holy Spirit with signs and wonders following, then *ask!* If you want the glory of His presence resting on your life, then *ask* for it and it will be yours!

2. Get in Your Place

God prophesied to us in the Old Testament through the lives of the patriarchs, the prophets, Moses, and Israel, revealing prophetic pictures of what was to come through Jesus Christ. I think the story of Moses reveals so much about the glory, the anointing, and the believer as New Testament temples of the Holy Spirit.

There is a beautiful picture in Exodus 40 that reveals the importance of being rightly positioned and anointed. Moses had just erected the tabernacle, and he was commanded to arrange the furnishings. Upon putting everything in its proper place, he anointed the furnishings to be set apart for the Lord.

> *And you shall take the anointing oil, and anoint the tabernacle and all that is in it; and you shall hallow it and all its utensils, and it shall be holy* (Exodus 40:9 NKJV).

My point here is that in order for you to receive the anointing of the precious Holy Spirit, you must be in your place. If God has called you in this season to be in the marketplace, lead a home group, attend a prayer meeting, or raise your kids, then this is right where you need to be. Do not despise the day of small beginnings. God sees your faithfulness, and it's in the place of stewardship where you find the anointing flowing.

I see so many people who want to preach to thousands, but they won't preach to one. I've seen those who want to prophesy to nations, but they won't give a word of encouragement to someone at the grocery store. We must be in our place faithfully if we are going to be anointed. Maybe you are greeting at your local church, helping as an usher, or faithfully giving. Keep going! God sees you!

Before David was king of Israel, he was stewarding sheep for his father's house. David was in his place of stewardship when the prophet Samuel anointed him with oil as the next king. The Bible says that when Samuel anointed David, the Holy Spirit came upon him from that day forward (see 1 Samuel 16:1-13).

It is high time that we ask the Lord what our current place of stewardship is. As we get in our place, God will pour out His precious anointing oil upon us. When we steward the place that God has given us and the measure of anointing that we currently possess, it is then that we will be given more.

I remember long before Miriam and I were traveling the world, the Lord told us to host a Bible study at our home. As we faithfully stewarded the 35 people in our home, God's anointing came. We taught, we prophesied, we prayed, and we hosted the presence of the Lord in our small home group faithfully for quite some time. We had no idea that our stewardship of the measure that we had been given would lead to a worldwide ministry! What you're currently stewarding in life, no matter how small or big, is preparing you for the more that God intends to pour out on your life! Get in your place and let the anointing flow! As the anointing begins to flow, it will begin to multiply!

3. Buy Oil

Then the kingdom of heaven shall be likened to ten virgins who took their lamps and went out to meet the bridegroom. Now five of them were wise, and five were foolish. Those who were foolish took their lamps and took no oil with them, but the wise took oil in their vessels with their lamps. But while the bridegroom was delayed, they all slumbered and slept.

And at midnight a cry was heard; "Behold, the bridegroom is coming; go out to meet him!" Then all those virgins arose and trimmed their lamps. And the foolish said to the wise, "Give us some of your oil, for our lamps are going out." But the wise answered, saying, "No, lest there should not be enough for us and you; but go rather to those who sell, and buy for yourselves" (Matthew 25:1-9 NKJV).

The bottom line here is that it is time to buy the oil of intimacy with the Lord, and the cost is your life. Fellowship with the person of the Holy Spirit is needed in this hour. Learning to know the Lord will cost you your time, your focus, and your obedience. There are no shortcuts to obtaining this costly but precious oil. We have got to get fresh oil daily! It is the fresh oil that multiplies the anointing in our lives. *"I shall be anointed with fresh oil"* (Psalm 92:10 KJV).

You and I cannot borrow someone else's oil of intimacy. We've got to go and get our own! We must be willing to lay our life down daily for the one who laid His down for us. He is altogether worth it.

4. Go! Use What You've Got!

There was a woman in the Bible who had just lost her husband and was in the process of losing everything she owned. The creditors were knocking at her door and wanted her two sons as payment. This distraught woman inquired of the Lord through the prophet Elisha and asked, "What must I do?"

Have you ever been there before? I know I have. Whether it be a much-needed miracle or just longing to walk in the fullness of our calling, I am sure that we can all say we've been right where this widow was at one time or another. She was desperate and she needed the God of miracles to break in. There is a power key in this story that I believe is essential to moving into greater measures of glory, miracles, and anointing. I honestly believe that we can even apply this principle to every aspect of our lives and see God break in every time.

> So Elisha said to her, "What shall I do for you? Tell me, what do you have in the house?" And she said, "Your maidservant has nothing in the house but a jar of oil."
>
> Then he said, "Go, borrow vessels from everywhere, from all your neighbors—empty vessels; do not gather just a few. And when you have come in, you shall shut the door behind you and your sons; then pour it into all those vessels, and set aside the full ones."
>
> So she went from him and shut the door behind her and her sons, who brought the vessels to her; and she poured it out. Now it came to pass, when the vessels were full, that she said to her son, "Bring me another vessel" (2 Kings 4:2-6 NKJV).

When she used what she had, God multiplied oil! It is time for us to use what we have been given and go if we are going to see the oil of God multiplied in our lives. We must not let feelings of inadequacy keep us from moving forward and using the gifts that He has placed inside us. When we use the current measure of grace that we have been given, we activate a supernatural multiplier in our life. When the apostles received the baptism of the Holy Spirit and started to preach the gospel, the Bible says that *"the Lord added to the church daily those who were being saved"* (Acts 2:47). Then in Acts 6 we see the number of disciples started to *multiply*. They went from addition to multiplication! Why? Because they used what they had!

One of my favorite revivalists in revival history was a woman by the name of Maria Woodworth-Etter. God used her mightily in her day. She moved in the power of the Holy Spirit and was used in revival in her generation. Two things almost stopped her before she even began. One: she didn't know the Bible and had never attended a Bible school. Two: it was not popular for women to be preachers in her day. Instead of letting those two opposing factors keep her from her purpose, she decided to go and use what she had despite her feelings of inadequacy. Because she decided to obey, go, and use what she had, Maria went down in revival history as one of the most powerful vessels God used during her time.

As someone once said, "God does not call the qualified; He qualifies the called." As we pray, obey, and go using what God has given us, He will qualify our calling, propelling us into multiplication.

5. Get Around Others Who Carry Glory

I cannot stress this principle enough. There is something extremely powerful about receiving from others through divine impartation. Divine impartation has the power to give you access to realms of God that others have paid a price for. My life has been changed greatly because I made a decision to get around others who were carrying something that I didn't have. The very breakthrough that you need might be resting upon someone else's life.

In the next chapter, I will talk more about accessing the power of God through divine impartation.

Let's pray:

> Lord, thank You that You have given me access to Your glory through the precious blood of Jesus. Help me to buy the oil of intimacy daily and learn how to use every gift that You have given me so that my life may bless someone else. Amen.

CHAPTER 7

The Power of Receiving Divine Impartation

Now Joshua the son of Nun was full of the spirit
of wisdom, for Moses had laid his hands on him.
—Deuteronomy 34:9 NKJV

It seems just like yesterday when Miriam and I decided to move two thousand miles from Texas to Redding, California, to follow the Holy Spirit's leading for our lives. We were hungry for more of God and we knew that adjustments in our life needed to be made in order for us to experience the more that God had for us. *Sometimes in order to go places in God that you have never been before, you've got to do some things you have never done before.* When you and I decide to hear and obey the Holy Spirit no matter the cost, it is then that we will discover *the more* that He has for us. Hearing and obeying are not only key but required in order to move into new realms of God.

A few months later, we were living in Redding and I was sitting in Bible class listening to a man I had never heard before lecturing on the baptism of love. This man's name was Randy Clark.

Randy began to tell a story of a time in his life when his lack of personal experience with God led him to longing in his heart for more. He went on to share that his desperation compelled him to drive several hundred miles away from his hometown to experience what God was doing through a man by the name of Rodney Howard-Browne.

There are two things you need to understand about revival. One: it is sovereign. Two: it will always come through a man or woman of God. Throughout Scripture and revival history, you see this happening. God always looks for a man or woman who is willing to be used as a vessel in the earth to bring forth God's revival. The book of Judges is a perfect example of this. Every time there was a decline in Israel, God would raise up someone as a vessel to bring forth His revival in the land. God has done this throughout history and is still doing it this way today.

Rodney Howard-Browne was one of those vessels. God was using him powerfully during the 1990s to spread revival fires throughout America and still is to this day. Randy knew he needed to be in one of Rodney Howard-Browne's meetings. He was a desperate man hungry for God and was willing to pay any price to encounter God, even if it cost him a long-distance drive.

Randy shared his story of how he stood in the prayer line to receive impartation. After not feeling much during the impartation time, he wondered if he had received anything at all. The great end and beginning of Randy's story is that this unsatisfied Baptist pastor actually did receive something that day, and he went on to be used as the catalyst of the great Toronto Outpouring of 1994.

While Randy was sharing all of this, my heart began to burn and tears began to run down my face. Something was happening deep within me. I sobbed and wept for hours, encountering the weighty love of God. The weight of God's love during that moment was so strong that I could not stand in my own strength. The only posture that felt appropriate was face down. Jesus was in the room and I knew it. The presence of the Lord was so tangible at that moment, and I didn't want to leave. I didn't care what I looked like or how I sounded; I just did not want to leave that moment. I could have stayed there in that glory forever. Randy never physically laid hands on me but I was definitely receiving something so deep.

It was like God was transferring something to me that Randy possessed that God wanted me to have. When I came out of that encounter, I knew something was different. I felt different. I felt closer to Jesus than ever before in my life. This encounter actually became very catalytic in launching me into where I am today as a revivalist. Since this defining moment, like Randy, God uses me in the ministry of impartation, revival, and the working of miracles.

DEFINING IMPARTATION

So what happened to me as Randy was sharing his story? I was receiving a divine impartation. I had just been upgraded into a new realm of God that I had not been in prior to class starting that day. *The ministry of impartation is absolutely necessary in order for us to step into new realms of glory.* I personally have received many times over the years from other anointed men and women of God who are being used for the ministry of impartation. I am eternally grateful for moments like these, because they have launched me into a world of power, miracles, and revival glory. As you posture yourself to receive the ministry of impartation from the Holy Spirit, it will not only change your life; it will activate new gifts of the Spirit, anointings, authority, and even new mantles.

Now, something I want to make clear before we go any further is that ministry of impartation is not just a prayer that you receive. I love prayer, but it's not just that. One impartation from God will do for you what 50 years of receiving prayer could never do. If anything, it is like a prayer on steroids!

It also isn't something that you receive from any man or woman. Just like I or anyone else for that matter cannot save you or heal you, neither can anyone transfer a special anointing from God to you. However, God does use people in the ministry of impartation as modes of transportation to dispense His anointing.

Impartation, simply put, is a transfer of the anointing of God that comes to you through someone else. It is how we receive the anointing that God wants us to have to carry His glory. Impartation is God giving you something that you do not currently possess. Again, it is God transferring greater measures of authority, power, access, grace, and glory to you personally. We see God doing this in Scripture with Moses and the elders of Israel:

So the Lord said to Moses: "Gather to Me seventy men of the elders of Israel, whom you know to be the elders of the people and officers, over them; bring them to the tabernacle of meeting, that they may stand there with you. Then I will come down and talk with you there. I will take of the Spirit that is upon you and will put the same upon them; and they shall bear the burden of the people with you, that you may not bear it by yourself alone" (Numbers 11:16-17 NKJV).

When you receive divine impartation, you are moving from one realm of glory to another. We also see this happening with Jesus's disciples when He imparted to them in Luke 9:1 (NKJV): *"Then He called His twelve disciples together and gave them power and authority over all demons, and to cure diseases."* What happened to them?

They received divine impartation from the Father through the life of Jesus so that they would be effective in their God-given assignment.

This is what God is doing at this very moment in history. Like Moses and Jesus, God is taking the same Spirit that is upon individuals who carry glory and anointing others. The days are over when only a select few carried the Spirit of glory, power, and revival. God is anointing and raising up a generation of glory carriers who have said yes to this divine call.

VEHICLES OF IMPARTATION

Anytime God gets ready to anoint you, upgrade you, or promote you, He will always bring someone to impart it to you. As mentioned earlier, revival as well as impartation will most often always come through a man or a woman. Someone who has received an authentic impartation can release it to others. It's just the way it works.

When addressing the church in Rome, Paul said, "*For I long to see you, that I may impart to you some spiritual gift, so that you may be established*" (Romans 1:11 NKJV). Paul was essentially saying, "I long to be with you so that I can give you something that the Lord wants you to have."

It is absolutely necessary for you to do whatever you can to get around those who are walking in the anointing. It may cost you your time, a move, a drive, or even money to travel somewhere. Miriam and I have done this over the years and still do it to this day. Why? Because our lives have been forever changed by it. Do whatever you need to do to position yourself to receive. When we receive the ministry of divine impartation from others, it establishes us and positions us to step into greater realms of glory.

KEYS TO RECEIVING DIVINE IMPARTATION

I want to be clear that impartation is not someone waving a magic wand over your head and *poof*—you start walking in power and new glory. It's not that at all. Nor should impartation be thought of as a removal of personal responsibility for study of the Word, walking in holiness, or pursuit of the Lord.

We must know that if we are going to receive anything from the Lord it will always require something from us. I love what Bill Johnson says: "The gospel is free, but maturity is expensive." I would agree. With this said, receiving the ministry of divine impartation starts a process within us that positions us to grow into the very thing that God has placed upon our lives.

1. First, we must learn to reach out and touch the anointing through faith and expectation.

Everything that we receive from God requires faith and expectation to access it. Jesus Christ died on the cross for our sins so that we will be saved but faith is required in order for us to obtain it. Faith is the key that unlocks the supernatural and invites the God of the impossible to invade our lives. Without faith it is impossible to even please God (see Hebrews 11:6). Faith and expectation are the two ingredients that make a demand on the anointing. A great example of someone who operated in faith and expectation is the story of the woman with the issue of blood in the Bible.

> *But as He* [Jesus] *went, the multitudes thronged Him. Now a woman, having a flow of blood for twelve years, who had spent all her livelihood on physicians and could not be healed by any, came from behind and touched the border of His garment, And immediately her flow of blood stopped.*
>
> *And Jesus said, "Who touched Me?"*
>
> *When all denied it, Peter and those with him said, "Master, the multitudes throng and press You, and You say, 'Who touched Me?'"*
>
> *But Jesus said, "Somebody touched Me, for I perceived power going out from Me"* (Luke 8:42-45 NKJV).

I would like to suggest here that it is possible to be in the same room with Jesus or even someone who carries the anointing and still receive absolutely nothing! We see this mentioned in the story above. Many were touching Jesus but only one made a demand on the anointing and received something from Him. In order for you to receive what God wants you to have, you must learn to reach out and touch the anointing through faith and expectation.

Expectation is one of the main keys to receiving. Expectation is what makes the demand on the very thing that we are believing for by faith. Faith and expectation go hand in hand. I have personally ministered in places where there was little expectation among the people and very little happened in the meeting. I have also been in places where people had so much expectation that I could literally feel the demand being made from the anointing on my life, which resulted in great glory being poured out. I have witnessed this with the miraculous as well.

For example, I was ministering in São José dos Campos, Brazil, and a woman came up to me who had a pelvic condition that caused her excruciating pain as well as a limp. As she approached me, I could tangibly perceive her faith and her expectation to be healed. When she asked me for prayer, I simply said, "Be healed in Jesus's name." That was it. There was no long contending prayer whatsoever. She was healed instantly at that moment. Why? She made a demand on the anointing through faith and expectation. Whatever it is that you need to fulfill your assignment, whether it be a personal miracle or God's precious anointing, you can access it now through faith and expectation.

Let's pray this prayer together:

> *Lord, I ask that You will increase my faith and expectation so that I can apprehend all that You have for me. Help me, Lord, to learn to make regular demands on the anointing so that I can receive new levels of glory that You have called me into in Jesus's name. Amen.*

2. Second, we must learn to discern the anointing.

To discern simply means to distinguish or to recognize. Being able to recognize the anointing when it is in operation is another vital key to receiving the ministry of divine impartation. Unfortunately, not everyone who ministers in the name of the Lord carries the anointing. I don't know what's worse—listening to someone minister who carries no anointing or not being able to recognize the anointing on someone who does.

In my opinion, one of the biggest pitfalls that can cause you to miss the anointing is familiarity. Do not become too familiar with those around you. The very breakthrough that you need may be sitting right next to you! People in Jesus's hometown missed their moment because they were too familiar with Jesus. The Bible says that He could do no mighty works in His hometown because of their unbelief in Him (see Matthew 13:58). They did not recognize the anointing of God's anointed.

I always want to make sure that I acquaint myself with the anointing so that when it is flowing I quickly recognize and respond accordingly. When I'm around someone who is ministering, I make sure not to look so much at the person or their ministry style but to look for the anointing. So many times we tend to write someone off because they don't minister in a way that we think they should.

Again, whatever your personal ministry flavor is, I want to warn you here to not look at the vessel but look for the oil in the vessel so you won't miss your moment. May our internal discerner be amplified so that our spirit man is fully aware when the anointing is present.

One of my spiritual fathers, Dan Duke, has always taught me anytime I get an internal impression that the anointing is in operation, I must position myself to give some kind of eternal expression in order to receive.[1] In other words, I will physically posture myself in such a way so that my triune being—spirit, soul, and body—is fully present while the anointing is flowing. For instance, when I sense the anointing in operation, I will quietly pray in tongues or turn the affections of my heart toward the Lord. I may even lift my hands as a sign of surrender and honor to the Lord during this time. By doing this, I now have become fully engaged with what God is releasing, thus positioning me to fully receive.

3. Third, we must hunger and thirst for the anointing.

One of the things that I learned a few years ago about spiritual hunger is that it doesn't originate from us. I've heard so many preachers say to others, "You just gotta be hungry in order to receive from God." Yes, that is true but you and I cannot make ourselves hungry for anything. Just like we cannot make ourselves hungry in the natural, we cannot make ourselves hungry for those things that are spiritual. I started praying several years ago that God would make me hungry for the things He wanted me to have, and sure enough He has!

If you're hungry for the things of God, it is God who has made you hungry. Your hunger is the supernatural grace of God upon your life to bring you into the very thing that you're hungering for. Hunger is a sure sign that you are about to experience the very thing that you're hungry for. The great news is that God will never bring you to His banqueting table hungry to eat and not feed you.

Years ago, Miriam and I became desperately hungry for God to use us in the miraculous as well as revival. Our hunger led us to study, pray, believe, and receive to see revival as well as the miraculous operate in and through our lives. As our hunger grew, we began to see revival break out in places that we visited, and we started to see many people supernaturally healed. This hunger for the miraculous as well as revival has now launched us into an international ministry where we hold revival gatherings and miracle services all around the world. Why? Because God made us hungry.

If you're hungry to be used in revival like us or to walk in the anointing, my friend, it is God who has made you hungry. If you're hungry to walk in signs, wonders, and miracles and to be used to change the world, it is God who has made you hungry. If you're hungry for any spiritual thing right now, it is because God intends to give it to you!

Your hunger is your invitation. Your hunger is your calling, your permission, and your commission to step into the very thing that you are hungry for.

Now that we understand how to receive divine impartation, let's look at God's different methods of transfer.

Let's pray:

> *Lord, thank You that You are releasing upon my life a fresh anointing. Lord, guide me to places and people You are using in this hour who have something to give me for this next season of my life. Thank You, Lord, that it is Your good pleasure to give to me fresh anointing, new authority, and increased power for Your name's sake. Amen.*

NOTE

1. Dan Duke and Mark Shubert, *The Impartation, Receive More from the Power of God* (Revival Publishing, 2021), 12, 25, 33.

CHAPTER 8

DISPENSING GOD'S POWER

Then He called His twelve disciples together
and gave them power and authority over all
demons, and to cure diseases. He sent them to
preach the kingdom of God and to heal the sick.
—LUKE 9:1-2 NKJV

We discussed in the last chapter how to position ourselves to receive divine impartation. Again, simply put, impartation is a divine transfer from God to you through someone else. It is God giving you authority, power, gifts, and abilities to fulfill your God-given assignment. Impartation can also be receiving something specific that is needed, like a miracle, healing, breakthrough, or deliverance.

Whether receiving or releasing impartation, there are modes of transportation that God uses to dispense His power.

LAYING ON OF HANDS

I personally have received impartation by the laying on of hands many times. One particular time was when Miriam and I heard that Rodney Howard-Browne was going to be ministering in a city near us. As we arrived, we could feel the expectation in the air. Rodney began to preach and flow with the Holy Spirit ministering to others in the room. Toward the end of the service, Rodney announced that he would be laying hands on everyone who wanted personal impartation. Miriam and I were so hungry. We knew it was time for us to be upgraded, and we were expectant to say the least. As we stood shoulder to shoulder next to others in the prayer line, we could hear Rodney getting closer to us as he announced with a forceful tone over those receiving impartation, "Fire!" Hungry people were falling down everywhere receiving the fire of God, and we too were ready to receive that fire! As soon as Rodney laid hands on Miriam and me, we both immediately came under the power of God, which caused us to fall to the floor. We lay there for quite some time just receiving what God wanted us to receive.

If you ever fall under the power of God, don't get up too quickly. I see this all too often. People want to get up immediately in fear of what they look like to others. Who cares?! I want what God has for me more than what people think! Many times you can miss what God wants to show you or speak to you during your time on the floor. Just stay there and receive until you sense that God is through with you.

After this impartation with Rodney, I began to notice that I had a new boldness, authority, and power when I preached. It was as though the measure of anointing that I had possessed was now multiplied. I noticed that when I prayed for others by the laying on of hands, most everyone I prayed for came under the power of God—unable to stand because of the weightiness of God's presence.

One such instance was when I was ministering in Blue Eye, Missouri, for *The Jim Bakker Show*. As I began to preach on joy, people all over the room became intoxicated with God's presence, resulting in holy laughter. One of those in attendance was a fifteen-year-old girl whom God really highlighted to me. I began to prophesy over her about the call of God on her life as a missionary to the nations. As I continued to prophesy over her, I felt led to lay my hands upon her to confirm what God was doing. Upon laying my hands on her, she came under a heavy anointing and she could not stand. Two hours later, her family had to carry her out because of the weight of glory that was on her.

Before receiving from Rodney, none of this happened to me when I ministered. Now this happens to me everywhere I go all over the world. I have ministered now to thousands by the laying on of hands, seeing many people experience God's weighty glory by it. Again, this all started in one divine impartation by the laying on of hands by another.

Laying on of hands is one of the primary methods that God uses to transport His power. We see that laying on of hands is actually an elementary teaching of the New Testament church (see Hebrews 6:2). We also see that God used this same method in the Old Testament as a means to transfer blessing, inheritance, anointing, authority, and even divine wisdom for leadership.

Now Joshua the son of Nun was full of the spirit of wisdom, for Moses had laid his hands on him (Deuteronomy 34:9 NKJV).

We see this mode of transmission being used to baptize the New Testament believers in the Holy Spirit as well.

Now when the apostles who were at Jerusalem heard that Samaria had received the word of God, they sent Peter and John to them, who, when they had come down, prayed for them that they might receive the Holy Spirit. For as yet He had fallen upon none of them. They had only been baptized in the name of the Lord Jesus. Then they laid hands on them, and they received the Holy Spirit (Acts 8:14-17 NKJV).

I heard Pastor Bill Johnson share a story of a time when a prophet friend of his, James Maloney, was seeing God miraculously dissolving metal in people's bodies. Bill, who understood the power of impartation, asked James to pray for him that he would begin to see this same type of miracle within his own ministry. Not long after, Bill began to see God supernaturally remove metal within peoples' bodies just as James had seen.

As soon as Miriam and I heard this testimony, we made sure to position ourselves to receive this measure of grace that Bill had received. Bill laid hands on the both of us, as well as others, that we might begin to experience this same miracle breakthrough in our own lives. This one impartation activated us into a whole new dimension of creative miracles. Now Miriam and I see God dissolve metal in people's bodies on a regular basis all around the world. This is the power of divine impartation through the laying on of hands.

Again, one who has received an impartation can release it to others. The measure of grace and anointing that we receive is not meant for us alone. We all have a responsibility to give away what God has freely given us. When we do, we show God that not only can we be entrusted as good stewards but we also position ourselves to receive even more! Jesus made this clear when He gave His disciples instructions for their assignment.

> *And as you go, preach, saying, "The kingdom of heaven is at hand." Heal the sick, cleanse the lepers, raise the dead, cast out demons. Freely you have received, freely give* (Matthew 10:7-8 NKJV).

We have been mandated by God to give away what we have received from the Lord. *What God imparts to us is meant to go through us to someone else.* We are called to let rivers of God run through us, *not* just to us. And one of the ways that rivers flow through us is by the laying on of hands.

One of my spiritual fathers, Dan Duke, told Miriam and me once, "There is a whole lot of preaching going on and not enough releasing. Make sure that when you minister to others to give them something eternal. That something, which is impartation, is the fruit that will remain." Miriam and I took this to heart, and we make sure to make room for impartation everywhere we go. In fact, this has become one of our main ministries along with the working of miracles.

Here is one of the many testimonies of the power of divine impartation from a man who attended one of our services:

> I remember the very first time I attended Tommy and Miriam's Saturday Night Awakening service at Trinity Church in Cedar Hill, Texas. The very first

night that we were there not only changed my life forever but my entire family as well. I witnessed my wife get physically healed that night, and I was baptized in the Holy Spirit for the first time. In addition to receiving the baptism of the Holy Spirit, I also experienced something I had never experienced before. I fell under the power of God's weighty presence for the very first time. I told my wife not to talk to anyone about what had happened until I could spend time reading the Bible. I spent the next several days in the Bible and researching what had happened to me. It was truly the most incredible and peaceful feeling I've ever had in my entire life. As we pulled into the driveway that night, my wife said, "Wow, I really needed that all week." I remember responding to her, "I've needed that my entire life!" That night was the beginning of what many people would consider supernatural acceleration. Our lives have been forever changed! We consider Pastors Tommy and Miriam spiritual parents because we have received so much from them. It has been almost three years since that first night, and I now anticipate the Holy Spirit will use me to share the love of Jesus wherever I go. I also would like to testify that I have personally received the impartation of boldness and joy from Pastors Tommy and Miriam. This past Sunday for the first time, I shared my personal testimony and preached the Word of God to a small church here in Texas. Thank You, Jesus, for the entire Evans family!

Jim How, Mansfield, Texas

PROPHECY

Prophecy is an extremely powerful way to receive impartation. Again, like laying on of hands, there is a biblical precedent for receiving impartation this way. Paul encouraged his spiritual son Timothy when he said:

> *Do not neglect the gift that is in you, which was given to you by prophecy with the laying on of the hands of the eldership* (1 Timothy 4:14 NKJV).

The prophet Samuel prophesied to Saul, saying,

> *The Spirit of the Lord will come powerfully upon you, and you will prophesy with them; and you will be changed into a different person* (1 Samuel 10:6 NIV).

This is exactly what happened. When Saul came around the other prophets, he was turned into another man at that moment and prophesied with them. Like young Timothy, Saul received an impartation through prophecy. True prophecy is extremely powerful. Not only does God declare your future but He causes it by imparting His divine power for you to walk in it. Anytime you receive an authentic prophecy, know that you are not only being encouraged but you're being equipped as well!

Miriam and I have the wonderful privilege of having Cindy Jacobs as a spiritual mom to us. Cindy is an international prophet who carries an anointing for revival at her core. Over the years, Miriam and I have received several prophetic words from Cindy that have been very catalytic for our lives as well as our ministry.

One such word was when Larry Sparks came to minister at one of our revival gatherings in February 2020. At that time, Miriam and I really didn't know Larry but we trusted the Holy Spirit's leading to have him come. We had no idea what was in store for us all that night. It just so happened that Cindy and Mike Jacobs were in town that Saturday night and decided to come to the service.

As Miriam and I began to minister in the service that night, the Holy Spirit came in like a swirling wind. We felt led to invite Cindy up at that moment, and she began to do what she does best—she jumped into the swirl with us! She pulled Larry, Miriam, and myself up together and she began to prophesy, "The Lord says, 'I have put you three together to re-dig the wells of revival in America.'"

As she ministered to us prophetically, we all came under the heavy power of the Holy Spirit. What was happening to all of us? We were receiving an impartation. Remember, an impartation from the Lord is God's permission and commission to do what He is calling you into.

Since then, Miriam, Larry, and I have traveled all over America re-digging the wells of revival. We have seen so many people over the last two years touched powerfully by the God of revival. Every time we go into a new city, there is a heavenly authority that comes with us. We continue to get testimonies back from the places that we have visited, and they all tell us that they are experiencing new levels of God like they never have before. Praise be the glory!

Not only has that one impartation given us power and authority to accomplish our assignment but it also knit us together with a new lifelong friend!

PROCLAMATION OF THE WORD

Proclaiming or preaching the Word is another means by which God will release divine power. Again, not everyone who preaches carries glory. Over the years I've heard a lot of good sermons from well-polished preachers who have a gift but no glory and no anointing, unfortunately. Like I said earlier, you can always tell when someone who is preaching carries glory. The whole atmosphere changes and everyone hearing the sound of their voice comes under the mighty influence of the Holy Spirit. It is in the atmosphere of anointed preaching that divine impartation is released.

The apostle Peter was one who carried an anointing for glory. Not only did people get healed when he walked by because of the glory that he carried, but they also got immersed in the Holy Spirit when he preached. This happened in the household of Cornelius, who was a centurion of the Italian Regiment.

> *While Peter was still speaking these words, the Holy Spirit fell upon all those who heard the word. And those of the circumcision who believed were astonished, as many as came with Peter, because the gift of the Holy Spirit had been poured out on the Gentiles also. For they heard them speak with tongues and magnify God* (Acts 10:44-46 NKJV).

What happened? As Peter preached the gospel to them, they came under the influence of the Holy Spirit and received His divine power. This little household received a divine impartation by anointed preaching! We must be a people who become so saturated with the anointing of the Holy Spirit that when we open our mouths the sound of heaven is released. The world does not need our polished, pitch-perfect sermons that carry no anointing. The world doesn't need a bunch of Ted Talk preachers who carry no fire and glory. What the world needs are preachers who open up their mouths and glory begins to manifest. As they open up their mouths, the whole atmosphere becomes saturated with God's presence, and His glory is now available for others to partake in.

Why? Because it is the glory that brings transformation, not intellectual sermons. If I preach anything at all, I want my preaching to be saturated with God's anointing oil. It's anointed preaching that destroys yokes, not my eloquent speech.

When someone who carries glory preaches, their preaching goes beyond time and space. In other words, it carries an anointing that becomes eternal. For example, I remember the very first time I heard Dan Duke preach was actually via YouTube months after he actually preached the sermon. It just so happened that he was preaching on impartation! As he began to preach on impartation, the atmosphere in my living room began to change. I felt the tangible, weighty presence of the Holy Spirit so strongly. As he continued to preach, deep guttural utterances began to flow from within me and I began to weep uncontrollably. I wept with tears of joy for over an hour. Again, something deep inside me was taking place. I was receiving a divine impartation. There was no hype. There was no loud music. Just an anointed preacher who carried glory.

We need anointed preachers now more than ever. Preachers who carry conviction, deliverance, miracles, and glory when they preach. When you recognize the anointing upon someone who is preaching, quickly open your heart and posture yourself to receive. I don't care how many times you have received from the Lord—remember there is always more.

ATMOSPHERIC IMPARTATION

Another way to receive impartation is by being within the atmo-sphere or environment of someone who carries glory. There are two ways to receive through atmospheres. The first way is by serv-ing someone who carries glory. Serving someone who carries glory, in my opinion, is an extremely powerful way to position yourself to receive. Miriam and I have made it a point to serve with honor others who carry glory.

> *Whoever welcomes a prophet as a prophet will receive*
> *a prophet's reward, and whoever welcomes a righteous*
> *person as a righteous person will receive a righteous per-*
> *son's reward* (Matthew 10:41 NIV).

In other words, when I honor or serve someone who carries a specific anointing, I tap into what they carry.

The second way to receive is by just being in the environ-ment or atmosphere of the person who is anointed for glory. For instance, many who visited the Brownsville Revival in 1994 received something eternal that changed the course of their lives forever. Many went on to become missionaries, evangelists, and preachers who went all over the world spreading revival. Others carried that same fire into the marketplace, turning the world upside down for God's glory. How? Those who received were those who postured their hearts to receive as they came into the atmosphere of God's glory that was being manifested.

This very thing happened with the prophet Samuel. He carried such an anointing of glory on his life that when others, includ-ing King Saul, got within close proximity of his atmosphere, they prophesied.

King Saul wanted to kill David because he became jealous of David and earlier in his life even rebelled against the Lord. David, who loved the Lord, fled to be with the prophet Samuel. As Saul sent messengers to apprehend David, they came under the influence of the Holy Spirit that was upon Samuel and they prophesied.

> *Then Saul sent messengers to take David. And when they saw the group of prophets prophesying, and Samuel standing as leader over them, the Spirit of God came upon the messengers of Saul, and they also prophesied. And when Saul was told, he sent other messengers, and they prophesied likewise. Then Saul sent messengers again the third time, and they prophesied also. Then he also went to Ramah, and came to the great well that is at Sechu. So he asked, and said, "Where are Samuel and David?"*
>
> *And someone said, "Indeed they are at Naioth in Raman." So he went there to Naioth in Ramah. Then the Spirit of God was upon him also, and he went on and prophesied until he came to Naioth in Ramah. And he also stripped off his clothes and prophesied before Samuel in like manner, and lay down naked all that day and all that night* (1 Samuel 19:20-24 NKJV).

Even our enemies can be apprehended by the glory upon our lives! This is so powerful for us to understand. You and I can get so saturated that we can carry an entire atmosphere filled with glory that affects those around us. As we grow in the anointing, we will grow in the glory. In other words, the atmosphere of glory that we currently carry can grow to where entire regions come under it.

This is exactly what happened in the story mentioned above. The city of Sechu was more than ten miles from the city of Naioth where Samuel resided. Saul came under the glory that was on Samuel over ten miles away! Again, not only can we receive for ourselves within the atmosphere of glory on the lives of others, but we too can carry it in such a way that entire regions are impacted.

DREAMS

Dreams are not typically a primary way that we receive impartation from the Lord, but He does use them as a way to impart to us. All of the other methods that are mentioned above are in partnership between God and His anointed vessels. However, dreams are 100 percent God imparting all by Himself. Now, not every dream comes with an impartation, but when they do it can be extremely powerful and life changing. The story of King Solomon is a great example of this happening.

> *At Gibeon the Lord appeared to Solomon in a dream by night; and God said, "Ask! What shall I give you?"*
>
> *And Solomon said: "You have shown great mercy to Your servant David my father, because he walked before You in truth, in righteousness, and in uprightness of heart with You; You have continued this great kindness for him, and You have given him a son to sit on his throne, as it is this day. Now, O Lord my God, You have made Your servant king instead of my father David, but I am a little child; I do not know how to go out or come in. And Your servant is in the midst of Your people whom You have chosen, a great people, too numerous to be numbered or counted. Therefore give to Your servant an*

understanding heart to judge Your people, that I may discern between good and evil. For who is able to judge this great people of Yours?"

The speech pleased the Lord, that Solomon had asked this thing. Then God said to him: "Because you have asked this thing, and have not asked long life for yourself, nor have asked riches for yourself, nor have asked the life of your enemies, but have asked for yourself understanding to discern justice, behold, I have done according to your words; see, I have given you a wise and understanding heart, so that there has not been anyone like you before you, nor shall any like you arise after you. And I have also given you what you have not asked: both riches and honor, so that there shall not be anyone like you among the kings of all of your days" (1 Kings 3:5-13 NKJV).

I too have received personal impartations from God within a dream. When I have encountered the Lord within those dreams, I have always begun to notice new levels of authority, power, and presence being released in and through my life. You too can ask God to impart to you within your dreams!

Let's pray:

Lord, I welcome every way that You want to release divine impartation to me. I open my heart now to receive. Holy Spirit, here I am, a child of Your affection. Fill me afresh again in Jesus's name. Amen.

CHAPTER 9

GOD'S VEHICLES: "KABOD GLORY FELT"

If Your Presence does not go with
us, do not bring us up from here.
—EXODUS 33:15 NKJV

MOVING IN THE MIDST OF THE GLORY

One of the most valuable things we can learn from our fathers and mothers of the faith in Scripture is that they made the presence of the Lord their priority. It was the glory that they longed for. Being with Him meant more to them than anything else. Moses was one of those men. God promised Moses that He would send one of His mighty angels before him as he took the land, but Moses wouldn't have it. He did not just want an angel; he wanted the glory. He

wanted the manifest presence of the Lord to go with him so much that he made a decision that he would not move unless the Lord went with him (see Exodus 33).

This decision not only impacted Moses but the entire nation of Israel. When the cloud moved, the entire nation would move. And when the cloud of glory settled, they would settle.

> *Then the cloud covered the tabernacle of meeting, and the glory of the Lord filled the tabernacle. And Moses was not able to enter the tabernacle of meeting, because the cloud rested above it, and the glory of the Lord filled the tabernacle. Whenever the cloud was taken up from above the tabernacle, the children of Israel would go onward in all their journeys. But if the cloud was not taken up, then they did not journey till the day that it was taken up* (Exodus 40:34-37 NKJV).

Anytime Israel settled in one place, it was because the glory had settled in that place. The place where they settled became a place of blessing, favor, abundance, and miracles. It was in that place that all went well. And it all went well because of the glory.

Ruth Ward Heflin makes a great point about moving in glory: "When the cloud lifted, it would not have been unusual for them to want to stay in that place of blessing. But the blessing is not in a place; it's in the cloud; it's in God's presence."[1]

In order for us to walk in the fullness of God's design for us and take hold of our inheritance as children of God, we must be found in the midst of the glory. God is looking for those who will not be satisfied with anything else but to be found by Him. It's in the realm of glory that we step into the fullness of our identity as image bearers of the Lord Jesus. To be honest, our lives as well as the lives of others depend on the glory.

WHY THE GLORY?

Again, the glory is the manifest presence of Jesus being made known. It is the realm of God's goodness and blessing. It is the realm of creative miracles and power where God invades the impossible.

When God manifests His glory, the realm of abundance, blessing, and acceleration is being made available. What would normally take years to accomplish in the natural world will only take a few months, weeks, or days in the glory. *The glory* is the realm of open heavens where angels ascend and descend. It is the realm of the outpouring of the Holy Spirit and revival. We need the glory now more than ever. And we cannot afford to move before it or behind it.

We must learn to move in the midst of the cloud (His glory) when it's moving and stay put when it has settled. Humanity is waiting in eager anticipation for the unveiling of sons and daughters of God who not only carry the glory but know how to move with it. It was absolutely vital and necessary for Israel's success to move with the glory, and it is the same for us today.

KNOWING GOD'S WAYS

In order for us to learn how to move with God's glory, we must first become familiar with His ways. Moses asked God to show him two things when God started to use him mightily as the nation's leader. He asked God, "Show me Your ways, that I may know You" and later asked, "Show me Your glory" (see Exodus 33:13,18).

There is a divine connection between knowing God's ways, knowing God, and the revealing of His glory. As we become better acquainted with the ways that God does something, we begin to recognize when He is moving. I think R. A. Torrey's words apply here again:

> Before one can correctly understand the work of the Holy Spirit, he must first of all know the Spirit himself.[2]

It is in the revealing of His ways that we come to know God more fully, thus giving us the ability to move along with Him.

VEHICLES OF GLORY

As mentioned in Chapter 2, God's glory is manifested as Kabod, which is felt, and Shekinah, which is seen. Throughout the years, Miriam and I have experienced both God's Kabod and His Shekinah. For the remainder of this chapter, I want to take time to not only show you some of the ways that God manifests His glory, but I also want to share testimonies with you that might help you learn to move with Him when receiving and releasing.

Glory Felt

Most often when God begins to manifest His glory, He will come with His weighty presence. This weighty presence will usually be tangibly discerned by your physical body as well as your mind, will, and emotions. These discernments would include, but are not limited to, vibrations, shaking, heat or cool sensations, falling down, tears, and holy laughter. These are signs that God is moving in our midst. When someone understands the ways in which the Holy Spirit can manifest, it will often open that individual's heart to receive more easily, thus moving with Him.

Unfortunately, instead of embracing the possible ways in which God manifests, most people either discredit them due to a lack of understanding or in some cases reject them entirely because they seem weird. Listen, if we are ever going to move into new realms of glory, then we've got to understand that God cannot be put into our tiny little boxes.

I have heard so many people say, "I don't want to look weird or embrace anything weird." I'm sure we have all said or thought this at one time or another in our lives. Can I propose something to you? I would like to suggest to you that God is weird. Now wait, before you throw my book in the trash and write me off as a heretic, let me explain and break it down.

One of the definitions for the adjective *weird*, according to the *Oxford English Dictionary*, is "to suggest something supernatural." God is supernatural. In other words, He transcends the laws of nature. All of humanity is longing for the supernatural because we are the offspring of a supernatural God! Most of what we would call weird is actually God's supernatural ways being put on display. From Genesis to Revelation, God does some pretty weird or supernatural things that go beyond our finite minds. He's God.

Think about it—a burning bush that is not consumed or a cloud by day and fire by night. Or what about heavenly manna on the ground? How about the Red Sea parting and consuming Israel's enemies or walls falling down in Jericho because of a holy shout of praise? What about the virgin birth, Jesus turning water into wine, or the apostle Paul sending out pieces of clothing that heal the sick? All weird.

Now, I am not saying let's just all be spooky Christians and embrace every little thing that comes our way. What I am saying is that if we are going to go higher in the things of God, then we must be willing to embrace those things that may go beyond our understanding or our level of personal experience. But some of you might be asking, "How do I know if the manifestation or encounter that I am experiencing is from God?"

A good way to know if a manifestation of God is authentic would be to look at the fruit or result of that manifestation. Is it consistent with the nature of God in Scripture? Does it bring people closer to Jesus and transfer the fruit that remains? Does it glorify God? If you can answer yes to any of these questions, then you can rest assured that the manifestation in operation is from God.

My dear friend Larry Sparks says, "I don't tolerate the manifestations of the Holy Spirit; I celebrate them." Again, if we are going to receive, minister, and move with the glory, then we have got to be okay with the ways in which God manifests. I never want to be one who rejects or scoffs at a manifestation just because I don't understand it or it's not happening to me.

Now I want to be clear concerning these supernatural manifestations. When God comes with His mighty supernatural power and manifests Himself among us, it is always to bless us. And that blessing always comes with a purpose. Everything He does has a purpose. It's never for us to just experience and go on our way. Any experience with God that we have is always meant to transform us and bring us into new realms of glory as well as make us effective in the Kingdom.

I want to encourage you not to be discouraged if you have not encountered these different types of manifestations personally yet.

I also want to embolden you to open yourself up to God and ask Him to give you all that He has for you no matter what mode of transportation He decides to use. More importantly, be strengthened today that you are learning about the different ways that the Holy Spirit manifests so you can partner with God, move with Him, and be a blessing to others.

Vibrations and Shaking

I personally have experienced vibrations and/or shaking many times in my own life as well as in those to whom I minister. Often this will feel like electrical currents or sensations that will start in the hands or feet. As one yields to what God is doing at this moment, it can be quite incredible as well as life changing. When this type of manifestation happens, it usually is indicative of the baptism of the Holy Spirit and fire coming upon you to prepare you for greater glory.

This type of manifestation has also been consistent for countless others throughout revival history. One such person was a healing evangelist by the name of John G. Lake. When describing an encounter he had with the baptism of God's fire, he journaled this:

> Then I became conscious of a change coming over me. Instead of the rain, currents of power were running through me from my head to my feet, seemingly into the floor. These shocks of power came intermittently, possibly ten seconds apart. They increased in voltage until, after a few minutes, my frame shook and vibrated under these mighty shocks of power. Then as I shook and trembled, the shocks of power followed each other with more apparent rapidity and intensity. My forehead

became sealed. My brain in the front portion of my head became inactive, and I realized the spirit speaking of His seal in their foreheads. I could have fallen on the floor except for the depth of the chair in which I sat.

Again a change. The shocks of power lessened in intensity and now have taken hold of my lower jaw. It moved up and down and sidewise in a manner new to me. My tongue and throat began to move in a manner I could not control. Presently, I realized I was speaking in another tongue, a language I had never learned. O, the sense of power. The mighty moving of the Spirit in me. The consciousness was God who had come.[3]

I am so thankful for people like Randy Clark, who has really taught a generation how to partner with God when He's moving on others. One of the things that I've learned from him is to pay attention to what God is doing as I minister to others and bless it. For instance, in this case, when God comes causing someone to tremble, because I know that the fire of God is upon them I will agree with the Lord and bless them with His fire. If it is joy, then I would bless them with joy. If healing, then healing. If tears, then love. It is my "yes and amen" in partnership with the Lord.

When we come to know the ways in which God manifests and choose to partner accordingly, it seems to be a multiplying effect that becomes a blessing to others. Now, God doesn't need us at all. He can bless anyone He wants to all by Himself at any time. However, God in His sovereignty chooses to partner with us to do His mighty exploits throughout the earth.

Heat and Cool Sensations

Most often, but not always, when someone feels heat or cool sensations, it is indicative of a healing anointing coming upon them. This can be felt both by someone needing a healing and by someone being used by God to dispense it. Many times during our healing and miracles services, people will testify that they feel heat coming upon them. When they experience this, we always encourage people by telling them that God's healing oil is flowing, so just receive.

Tears of Love

In my opinion, tears are one of the most precious vehicles that God uses because they are accompanied by a baptism of God's love. As mentioned in the first chapter, this was one of my first encounters with the Lord. When God baptizes us with His love, it will always be a deep work taking place within our hearts. The word *baptize* in the Greek is pronounced *baptizo*, which means to immerse or submerge repeatedly. It is God immersing us with His love over and over again. This has happened to me privately, corporately, as well as while I have ministered to others.

In 2021, Miriam and I were invited to join our dear friends Larry Sparks and Rebecca Greenwood in Kansas to minister alongside them at their Awakening the Well of Revival conference. The atmosphere was one of expectancy and excitement as we gathered to see what the Lord would do. As one of our friends, Jessi Green, began to minister, she invited Miriam and me up to help minister to the people. She felt that we were to take bottles of water and baptize people who were present in the meeting. As I began to minister to the people, I felt God's weighty glory begin to fall upon me. Tears of love began to run down my face as I took capfuls of bottled water and poured it out upon the heads of those in attendance.

As I went about pouring water on their heads, I felt such a deep love for each one of them. It was the deep love of God. As I continued, I noticed every single person I prayed for came under God's weighty love and began to weep uncontrollably. As God immersed all of them with His presence, some also fell under the power of His weightiness as they experienced God's tears of love. What did I do? I just continued to bless what God was doing, and in the process it blessed me. It was as though Jesus was loving them through me.

I believe God has created our emotions not just for our benefit but also for His. Since we are joined together in one spirit with the Lord, we can feel His heart for humanity as well as His love for us. Tears of love is a way in which God reveals His glory.

Falling Down

This phenomenon occurs when the weightiness of God's glory comes upon someone. Remember, one of the words for *glory* is the word *Kabod*, which means "weighty." When God's weighty glory comes upon us, it becomes hard to stand. Think about it—when the God of the universe touches our human bodies, there will be a response of some kind. I think it is absolutely incredible that as humans we can encounter God. But what's even more incredible than that is that we live through those encounters to talk about it. I have been in services when the Lord's weighty glory begins to fall in the room and you feel it! I don't know about you, but I want God's holy disruptions to fill the room with His glory! I believe a day is coming when God's glory will invade us in such a way during our worship gatherings that no one will be able to stand because of the weight of glory in the room.

I personally have experienced this many times in my life—I could not stand because of the weight of glory upon me. I have also seen thousands of those whom I have prayed for experience this same kind of glory. There have even been times when I am ministering in the glory that I can hardly stand myself as I minister. When this happens to me, almost everyone I pray for comes under that same weight of glory, resulting in them falling under the power. Again, this is a vehicle that God uses to reveal His glory. God has been consistently revealing Himself this way throughout biblical history.

When King Solomon was dedicating the temple, the priests could not stand to minister because of the glory.

> *And it came to pass, when the priests came out of the holy place, that the cloud filled the house of the Lord, so that the priests could not continue ministering because of the cloud; for the glory of the Lord filled the house of the Lord* (1 Kings 8:10-11 NKJV).

Here is a story of a 17-year-old boy who experienced God's weighty glory in one of our Saturday Night Awakening services.

> During one of Tommy and Miriam's Saturday Night Awakening services, I experienced a fresh outpouring of the Lord's joy. I walked in feeling sad and walked out feeling God's joy. I recall it being to the point where I had to ask God to help me position my heart to even worship Him. During worship, I stood at the front and raised my hands, praising Him. I stood there crying while feeling electricity in my hands and a sense

of peace like nothing could explain. Pastor Tommy invited the people who were experiencing holy manifestations—including electricity in the hands—to the front to receive the Holy Spirit. Because what I was experiencing was confirmed to me by God's usage of Pastor Tommy, I knew I had to go to the front. As I continued to worship God, my hands were shaking as I prayed to receive His Holy Spirit. As Pastor Tommy prayed over me, I remember my legs gave out as I was slain by the Holy Spirit. I could not move my body but I had so much peace. I lay there blissfully, laughing in joy in God's presence. What seemed like only minutes actually ended up being more than two hours until the service ended! Because of this encounter, whenever I think of an eternity worshiping God in heaven, this is what I think of.

ALEX HOWE
Cedar Hill, Texas, October 17, 2022

Joy through Holy Laughter

Joy, I believe, will be one of the main vehicles that God will use in these last days to release His glory. I will unpack this manifestation more fully in a later chapter, but I do want to include it here in the context of glory that is felt. Again, God who created our emotions will often manifest His glory to us and through us within the seat of our emotions. Joy through holy laughter can be extremely beneficial not only to your soul but also your physical body. It's actually quite intoxicating! In Acts 2 when the Holy Spirit was poured out on the 120 believers, there were observers who thought that those in attendance were all drunk (see Acts 2).

Joy through laughter is extremely powerful for shifting atmospheres over individuals as well as a corporate group of believers. The manifestation of joy can be found within the Bible as well as revival history. I personally have experienced this as well and have had the privilege of witnessing countless others experience this vehicle of glory, resulting in great eternal breakthroughs. Again, anytime I see God touching someone in this way, I just bless what He is doing.

Here is a testimony of one of our ministry leaders who has attended several of our services.

> I remember one particular Saturday Night Awakening when Tommy and Miriam were ministering. As Tommy began to minister, I began to laugh, which quite frankly was hard to control. I laughed continually for at least an hour. Not only did I laugh, but I would also hang on to others to impart that laughter to them. That night, I witnessed God pour out joy on not only me but so many others. It was like God poured out a bucket of joy! I can still see myself and my friend Jamie lying on the hard floor, holding tight to each other, but experiencing such a joy that could not be contained. The joy that I received that night has stayed with me ever since. It has allowed me to see how the joy of the Lord is so very important and just how generous God is. I would also like to give testimony that I was healed from deep wounds of the past that night. I now know that I must give away what I have received and pass that healing on to others.
>
> SUE MAINORD, Cedar Hill, Texas

"WHAT HAPPENS IF I DON'T FEEL ANYTHING?"

There is one more thing that I think is extremely important when it comes to receiving or releasing the glory of God. All of the above mentioned ways in which God touches the lives of others are definitely considered to be evidence of God dispensing His glory and power. However, you and I can still receive or release God's glory and not see any of these manifestations happen. *Our focus should never be on manifestations, but it must always be on Jesus. Jesus is our focus for all ministry.*

Again, we must never resist manifestations if they do occur or be embarrassed by them, but always welcome them. They are ways in which God reveals His glory and power. Neither should we ever manufacture or fake manifestations. Our job when receiving is to use our self-control to yield to the Holy Spirit, allowing Him to do whatever He wants to do. Our job when releasing is to learn to know and see what God is doing and to bless it.

I want to conclude this chapter with a story of a young man who was a student of ours. Anytime there was an opportunity to receive divine impartation, he was one of the first in line. Miriam and I have prayed for him several times without him experiencing any outward manifestations of any kind. So much so that he came to us wondering if there was something wrong with him. I encouraged him to not be concerned if he wasn't "feeling" anything but to know that he was in fact receiving something.

Later, when this young man was given the opportunity to be a part of the prayer team at his church, almost everyone he prayed for came under the power, causing them to fall to the floor by God's weighty glory. Even though he never really felt anything during his own pursuit of divine impartation, he still received and became a carrier of God's presence, for God had anointed him.

Now that we have identified some of the ways in which we can feel God's glory, let's discuss in the next chapter God's glory that is tangibly seen.

Let's pray:

> *Lord, help me to recognize when You are moving. Holy Spirit, help me to partner with You to advance the Kingdom to me and through me in Jesus's name. Amen.*

NOTES

1. Ruth Ward Heflin, *Revival Glory* (Hagerstown, MD: McDougal Publishing, 1998).

2. Torrey, *The Person and Work of the Holy Spirit*, 1.

3. John G. Lake, *The Complete Collection* (New Kensington, PA: Whitaker House, 2005), 78-80.

CHAPTER 10

SIGNS, WONDERS, AND MIRACLES: "SHEKINAH GLORY SEEN"

Here am I and the children whom the Lord has
given me! We are for signs and wonders in Israel
from the Lord of hosts, who dwells in Mount Zion.
—ISAIAH 8:18 NKJV

I want to start this chapter by telling you that you were made for signs, wonders, and miracles! You are the offspring of a supernatural God who longs for you to display His glory on the earth. Your credentials as a believer in Jesus Christ are signs, wonders, and miracles (see Mark 16:17-20). In addition, you have been commissioned by Jesus and empowered by the Holy Spirit to be a sign and wonder to a lost and dying world. By design, your life was created to reveal Jesus to the world and get the attention of those who don't yet know Him through signs, wonders, and miracles following.

When Moses was wandering around in the desert, the Bible says that he saw a bush that was on fire but was not consumed. Moses's curiosity caused him to step aside and see what the strange sight was all about. When Moses stepped aside to see, God spoke to him out of the midst of the bush. This is a picture of the New Testament believer. Your life is meant to be a burning bush that gets the attention of the curious. Once those curious ones step aside, they hear God from within the midst of your life!

I believe this is why the ministry of signs, wonders, and miracles must be front and center as we proclaim the good news of the gospel. Signs, wonders, and miracles are never meant to validate our ministry, but they are designed to validate the message of Jesus Christ. They are available to bring glory to Jesus and bring people into a loving encounter with His presence.

Signs, wonders, and miracles are the manifestation of the Shekinah glory that is tangibly seen. If we are going to move in and carry glory, then we have got to be accustomed to signs, wonders, and miracles. The early church gave us a biblical precedent for walking in signs, wonders, and miracles.

Now, Lord, look on their threats, and grant to Your servants that with all boldness they may speak Your word, by stretching out Your hand to heal, and that signs and wonders may be done through the name of Your holy Servant Jesus (Acts 4:29-30 NKJV).

> *And through the hands of the apostles many signs and wonders were done among the people* (Acts 5:12 NKJV).

> *And Stephen, full of faith and power, did great wonders and signs among the people* (Acts 6:8 NKJV).

A *sign*, according to Hebraic Scripture, means a distinguishing mark, banner, or miracle. Just as street signs point us in the right direction and give information that is necessary for any road trip, so do spiritual signs. They point us to Jesus.

A *wonder* is a special display of God's power that brings us into the awe and wonder of God. And a *miracle* would be God creating something out of nothing, defying natural laws. Again, all of these serve the purpose of revealing the nature, character, and beauty of Jesus.

In this chapter, I want to give you the different ways in which God shows us His glory through signs, wonders, and miracles as well as examples from Scripture and testimonies. Again, God will not be confined or contained. He's God. Because He's God, He could reveal His glory beyond the methods listed within this chapter.

Now, some of you may be asking yourself this question: "What if the sign and wonder that is experienced is from the devil?" I think Pastor Bill Johnson answers this question so beautifully: "If it's God, we worship God. If it's the devil, we worship God."

Again, look at the fruit of the manifestation. All true signs, wonders, and miracles will always bring you closer to Jesus.

GOLD DUST, GLORY CLOUD

I remember the very first time we as a family experienced what I would call a golden glory cloud. We had just driven two thousand miles from Texas to relocate to Redding, California, in hopes that what we thought we heard God say was actually Him speaking to us. To be honest, even with all of the confirmations, I still wasn't sure. We left our extended family, friends, business, and sold our home all because we felt God was speaking to us.

It was our very first weekend at our new church, and to be honest I was having second thoughts about being there. It wasn't the church; it was me. I kept asking questions like, "What in the world did we just do?" "Did we actually hear God speak?" "Did we miss it?" With all of these questions racing through my head, we decided as a family to go to the Friday night service at our new church, Bethel. It was getting late and Miriam and I had three little girls, so we decided to sit in the back row just in case we needed to slip out.

As worship continued, my youngest daughter, Lauren, began to get sleepy, and I felt the need to settle her in my arms. I decided that it might be best to go in the lobby and walk her back and forth until she fell asleep. As she began to doze off, I heard the Holy Spirit speak so clearly to me: "Get back into the sanctuary. I want to show you something." I quickly obeyed this prompting from the Lord.

As I entered the sanctuary, I began to notice golden specks of dust appearing one by one in the air above us. As I looked up at it, I thought my eyes were playing tricks on me. I nudged Miriam and asked her, "Did you see that?" She said, "Absolutely!" As soon as we both realized what was happening, a huge golden glory cloud began to form in the room. It began to swirl and billow above us all. Miriam, the girls, and I began to weep as we experienced God's deep love. I knew then that we had heard God speak and we were in the right place. This brought so much faith and encouragement to our hearts. We were convinced that God not only directed us, but He was with us on the journey!

Golden Glory Cloud: Saturday Night Awakening, Trinity Church

Seven years after our first encounter with God's golden glory cloud, Miriam and I were faithfully serving as pastors of the Saturday Night Awakening service at Trinity Church. Along with our incredible team, Miriam and I were contending and believing for a move of God at our church. We were all in for whatever God wanted to do. We didn't care what it could look like or what stigma might be attached to it—we just wanted the God of revival. As we gathered with our team before service to pray, we all felt that God would meet us powerfully as He had done in prior weeks. We were seeing people miraculously healed, filled with the Holy Spirit, and delivered from demons as well as the lost being saved. We were experiencing an awakening!

As we gathered that evening to worship, we could feel God's tangible presence in the room. While the worship team continued to lead us in song, my daughter Madison was on stage painting prophetically. For those of you who are not familiar with prophetic painting, it is a form of worship through the arts. As worship songs are sung, the prophetic artist will hear what God is speaking and paint what they hear or see God doing. My daughter Madison began to see a picture from the Lord of golden glory. As she began to paint what she was seeing, a gold dust cloud began to fill the air. It went from the back of the room all the way to the front of the stage, filling the entire room! We were in such amazement, to say the least! People were caught up in the awe and wonder of God, and we all experienced His goodness and love for us.

Here are two testimonies from that night:

There were many times during the Saturday Night Awakening service when the presence of the Lord was so strong. This was one of those particular nights. Everyone from the worship team, the prophetic artist, and every soul in the room had their hearts postured to the Lord. My personal experience of this night has been marked forever by specifically witnessing the manifestation of the glory of God. I have always heard about supernatural encounters in a corporate setting and believed it could happen at any moment. During worship you could tell words became love songs, and love songs became a groan. The presence of God flooded my heart and tears began to flow. I knew there was a cleansing in my heart taking place. To give the Lord my highest praise, I knelt on the floor as the tears were increasing. I imagined what the wise men felt being the first to present gifts to the newborn King. As I was engulfed in the Father's arms with my eyes closed, I could sense the supernatural activity increase in the room. Although I was aware of the beginning of a supernatural manifestation of the glory of God and wanted to lift my eyes to see, I knew leaving my current posture would be leaving a more tangible presence of the Lord. There came a time I felt the release from Abba to lift my head, and when I looked up it was pouring rain of gold dust coming down upon me. I immediately felt like I needed to duck for cover from the intensity of the pour. I was filled with joy immediately. Next to me was Pastor Tommy, and without any words we were just in awe of the presence in the room. I knew the Lord was speaking to me about the pour, as others in the room saw it as well. After this night I understood the meaning of "from glory to glory," which takes obedience from within. All glory to God!

CRYSTAL WULFF, Dallas, Texas

On March 24, 2018, during our weekly Saturday night service led by Tommy and Miriam Evans, "Show Us Your Glory" was being sung by the worship team. As I looked up, I saw a swirling cloud with sparkling glory manifest before my eyes. As I alerted my husband sitting next to me, he asked if I could feel it. Not only could I feel that tangible presence, but I could also feel His wraparound presence. I was in awe of what I was seeing and feeling and had never experienced anything like that before. Deep gasps and tears of others began as they noticed what was happening in this amazing presence.

Then a second cloud appeared in front of the drummer as he played. Another appeared in front of the sound booth as they literally felt the moisture hitting their faces. Gently that glory cloud moved from the front to the back of the sanctuary.

Completely immersed in the moment, I lost track of time but was forever marked by the kiss from heaven.

That unexpected, life-changing experience will remain with me as long as I live.

Lisa and George Haydin, Desoto, Texas

FEATHERS

Miriam and I have seen feathers falling while we minister in the flow of the Holy Spirit many times. This phenomenon happens either when we preach or when we are moving in miracles and deliverance.

I believe feathers are another way God manifests His glory and reveals His angelic activity. They are a sign of God's abiding presence and His divine protection in our midst.

> He who dwells in the secret place of the Most High shall abide under the shadow of the Almighty. I will say of the Lord, "He is my refuge and my fortress; my God, in Him I will trust." Surely He shall deliver you from the snare of the fowler and from the perilous pestilence. He shall cover you with His feathers, and under His wings you shall take refuge (Psalm 91:1-4 NKJV).

I remember a time when I was teaching in our prophetic school and I had put together a detailed outline of notes that I thought were important. As I began to teach, God totally hijacked the meeting and people began to encounter the joy of the Lord while experiencing heavy glory. I continued as best I could under God's weighty presence. There seemed to be such a flow of divine revelation that kept coming forth out of my mouth, and it was coming quicker than I could think it. These were things that I had never said before. The words that I was speaking were fresh off the press!

It was as though God was unlocking deep mysteries that were beyond my comprehension. I was honestly quite shocked because all of this came out of nowhere, with such ease and surprise. I had to go back later and try to write down all that God was speaking through me because it was all new to me.

Later that night after getting home, I noticed a feather hanging out of the bottom of my pant leg. I said to myself, "This explains why the night was so extraordinary!" God was there! Again, God was giving me a sign that He was with me and to trust His leading beyond my notes or intellect.

RAIN

Sometimes God will manifest His glory as a confirmation of a prophetic word being released. One such instance was when I was in Belo Horizonte, Brazil. I felt like the Lord had given me a word about a fresh outpouring of the Holy Spirit coming to Brazil. All morning I kept feeling rain drops falling on my face and hands as I worshiped in the service. As I got up to release the word, I felt a huge rain drop hit the top of my head. It was not raining outside and there were no clouds in the sky. God was confirming His Word by this supernatural sign of rain!

Another such instance was while Miriam and I were ministering in Kentucky at an outdoor event. We began to declare that God was bringing a fresh rain of outpouring to Kentucky. As soon as I said the words *fresh rain*, it started to rain. Everyone began to worship in the rain and did not want to leave. Miriam and I began to lay hands on people as they worshiped the Lord. There was such a peaceful and sweet presence that rested in that entire field. Keep in mind, there was no forecast of rain. No one could believe what was happening. When they looked at the radar, a small cloud appeared right over where we were at. All of the surrounding areas were completely dry with no rain. The cloud settled over this specific area and didn't move! The people of Kentucky were encouraged by this supernatural sign. God had confirmed His Word by this sign of rain.

SUPERNATURAL OIL

I personally have never yet experienced the manifestation of supernatural oil, but I still want to list it here because there have been some who have experienced it in our services. Anytime you read about God's holy oil in the Bible, it always signifies the anointing of the Holy Spirit, holy consecration, and power for service.

This supernatural manifestation of the oil is another way that God has revealed His glory throughout revival history as well as today.

In his book *The Miracle of the Oil*, Joshua Mills shares one of his experiences with supernatural oil:

> One afternoon that weekend, as I was in my hotel room preparing for the meeting, prayerfully searching the Scriptures and seeking God for what He wanted to do, I suddenly began to feel oil physically forming in the palms of my hands. As is typical when oil supernaturally comes in this way, I first saw it appearing in the crease of my hands. Other people might disregard such a manifestation or write it off as sweaty palms or natural oils, but I've learned to discern the holy presence of God in it. Immediately, my heart turned to the Lord to worship. I thanked

Him for what He was doing, and I invited the Spirit to increase the manifestation. I truly desire to be a vessel for the oil of God's presence, and I am always willing and eager for this miracle oil to flow in greater measure. As I was seeking God in prayer and adoration, asking what He desired to do in the meeting that evening, the miracle oil increased. Soon it filled my palms completely and began to drip off them onto my wrists and fingers. The oil kept flowing, gently pouring onto my arms. I was being surrounded by a heavenly fragrance that smelled more extravagant than the most luxurious perfume.[1]

Another testimony of the manifestation of supernatural oil that I want to share happened to a five-year-old boy by the name of Lavin Burcham. This young boy's testimony is actually what started this new manifestation of God's glory in the ministry of the late healing evangelist A. A. Allen. Here is a portion of the testimony that was given by the boy's mother, Mrs. Sander Burcham, which was published in *Miracle Magazine* in 1955.

Lavin had hardly laid down in bed when he began to shout praises of God and to speak in tongues. I knew that what was taking place was no commonplace experience. God was doing an unusual work. Then suddenly Lavin became very quiet. Big tears ran down his cheeks. Then suddenly he held out his hands. "Mother, Daddie! Look! Look at the oil Jesus is pouring on my hands!" he cried. "It isn't just plain oil. You can't buy this oil in the store. This is real oil, and it is coming from Jesus. Feel the oil, Mother and

Daddie!" He placed his hands upon my cheek and upon his father's cheek. We could feel the oil on our faces. "Oh Mother, Daddie, I can feel it all over me! Do you know what Jesus is telling me to do? He's telling me to take this oil and lay it on the sick and if they believe, they shall be healed."[2]

Why in the world would God do something like this? Because He is God and He does what He pleases (see Psalm 135:6). Again, we have got to learn to be okay with the unusual if we are going to be glory carriers in the earth. I want God and all that He has for me no matter what it may look like. You and I are meant to experience His precious glory in any way that it may come!

HEALINGS, MIRACLES, TONGUES, AND CASTING OUT DEMONS

I want to briefly include in this chapter healings, miracles, tongues, and casting out demons because they are in fact manifestations of the glory that you can tangibly see. Jesus referred to these signs in Mark 16:17-20. I discussed the diversity of tongues in Chapter 5, so I won't go into detail here. However, as a reminder, the diversity of supernatural tongues that I am referring to will manifest specific dialects that are supernaturally given by the Lord as a sign to the unbeliever (see 1 Corinthians 14:22).

Deliverance becomes really easy in the glory. When God's presence is tangible, demons leave! Instead of long deliverance sessions, demons come out with a command in the glory. Miriam and I have seen many people delivered of demonic strongholds within the midst of the glory with only a word. When people get free of demons, God's glory is seen and He is revealed as the Lord who sets captives free. "Now the Lord is the Spirit; and where the Spirit of the Lord is, there is liberty" (2 Corinthians 3:17 NKJV).

In the next chapter I will discuss in greater detail healing and miracles in the glory.

Let's pray together:

> *Lord, You are the Spirit of Glory and I welcome You. I ask that You will activate within me every good and perfect gift. I ask that through my life You will perform signs, wonders, and miracles so that Jesus can be glorified. Glorify Yourself through me, Lord. Teach me how to welcome and partner with You as You display Your power and reveal Your glory. Amen.*

NOTES

1. Joshua Mills, *The Miracle of the Oil* (New Kensington, PA: Whitaker House, 2022).

2. *Miracle Magazine: The Allen Revival News*, vol.1, no. 2, November 1955, 10.

CHAPTER 11

HEALING AND MIRACLES IN THE GLORY

And believers were increasingly added to the Lord,
multitudes of both men and women, so that they
brought the sick out into the streets and laid them
on beds and couches, that at least the shadow
of Peter passing by might fall on some of them.
—ACTS 5:14-15 NKJV

One of the things that Miriam and I burn to see God do is to manifest His loving kindness through the ministry of healing and miracles. I believe with all of my heart that the ministry of healing and miracles is central to the gospel. *Gospel* simply means "good news." It is good news that Jesus not only removed all of our sins

but paid for us to be healed. He is Christ our Savior, Deliverer, and Healer! He is Christ our Miracle Worker! Whatever you are believing God for today, Jesus paid for it on the cross so you could access it by faith.

God has been so faithful throughout the generations as He has released great miracles among us. I believe we as the body of Christ are stepping into the *greater works* that Jesus promised in John 14:12. I thank God for all that He has done and all that He is about to do, for He is faithful.

In this chapter, I want to talk about *healing and miracles* in the glory. First, however, I want to discuss some very important truths concerning miracles as well as share testimonies and various ways in which God releases those miracles. I believe that the testimonies within this chapter will prophesy over your life in Jesus's name! I declare that any measure of breakthrough in the realm of miracles that Miriam and I have received is yours to apprehend in Jesus's name! Take it!

Recently, I was in Belo Horizonte, Brazil, and I was about to minister to around five thousand hungry Brazilians. I knew in my heart that the Lord wanted me to move in the ministry of miracles and impartation. But how? I kept wondering, "How on earth am I going to lay hands on every single one of these people?" The building we were in had stadium-type seating with three levels and it was packed full. It would have been impossible for me to even consider laying hands on all of them, and I'm sure it would have been physically exhausting if I tried. After realizing this almost impossible task, I knew in my spirit that if God asked me to do something, then He must have a plan to get the job done. As I approached the stage to preach, I felt an impression of the Lord's voice in my spirit that sounded something like this: "You're going to minister in the glory."

As I began to preach what God had put on my heart, the atmosphere began to suddenly change. I felt the tangible presence and power of the Lord in the room, and so did everyone else! As the room filled with God's manifest presence, I invited all those who wanted more to lift their hands. As everyone in the building lifted their hands, the power of God came upon them all. People started rushing the platform and fell under the power of God. They were receiving divine impartation to carry God's fire and glory! Then the Holy Spirit directed me to release words of knowledge for healing. So many people were healed all because God's manifest presence was falling upon them. Tumors dissolved, hearing was restored, and barren wombs were opened!

Here is a testimony that came from a man by the name of Claudio Barreto regarding his wife's miraculous healing that day:

> In January of 2019, you came and ministered at the Clamor Prophetic Conference at the Lagoinha Baptist Church in Belo Horizonte. My wife was recently diagnosed by doctors that she would not be able to get pregnant and that she had multiple cysts on her ovaries. Ten days before the conference we went to a doctor, and this is what she said to my wife: "You have several cysts, and unfortunately you will never be a mother." We have spent a lot of money and my wife has been very depressed since we received the diagnosis. As you began to pray for people to be healed that day at the conference, we both knew in our hearts that she was healed. Deep down I never lost the faith that Jesus would do a miracle, and He

did! I want to testify that my wife has been supernaturally healed and she is three months pregnant!

Several months later, Claudio sent a picture of their new beautiful baby girl!

HEALING AND MIRACLES ARE PART OF GOD'S NATURE

The glory is the realm of creative miracles. This is the realm where impossibilities bend their name to the name Jesus! Sickness, disease, infirmity, affliction, and demons can't coexist in *the glory!*

Healing and miracles are another way that God shows us His glory. If you and I are going to steward a life of miracles, then there are some important truths that we must know in order to partner with the flow of God's presence.

Throughout Scripture, we find that God many times revealed Himself to Israel as the God who heals. *"I am the Lord who heals you"* (Exodus 15:26 NKJV). God spoke those words to about three million people! *"He also brought them out with silver and gold, and there was none feeble among His tribes"* (Psalm 105:37 NKJV). God brought some three million people into the promised land and none of them were afflicted or infirmed! Psalm 107:20 (NKJV) declares that, *"He sent His word and healed them."* We can conclude here that healing is a part of God's divine nature.

"JESUS CHRIST IS PERFECT THEOLOGY"

The first time I ever heard this statement from our pastor Bill Johnson was when I lived in Redding, California. Jesus is the perfect will of God revealed to mankind.

God, who at various times and in various ways spoke in time past to the fathers by the prophets, has in these last days spoken to us by His Son, whom He has appointed heir of all things, through whom also He made the worlds; who being the brightness of His glory and the express image of His person (Hebrews 1:1-3 NKJV).

He is the image of the invisible God, the firstborn over all creation (Colossians 1:15 NKJV).

Jesus told Phillip, "If you've seen Me, you have seen the Father" (see John 14:9). Jesus was and is the exact representation of the Father. If we want to know God's will concerning healing and miracles, we must look to Jesus. He is our model for all ministry and life.

IS IT GOD'S WILL TO HEAL?

If we are going to be carriers of the glory, where miracles are performed, then we must have no doubt in our minds of the will of God concerning healing and miracles. Again, we must look to Jesus to know God's perfect will.

Now a leper came to Him, imploring Him, kneeling down to Him and saying to Him, "If You are willing, You can make me clean." Then Jesus, moved with compassion, stretched out His hand and touched him, and said to him, "I am willing; be cleansed" (Mark 1:40 NKJV).

"When the sun was setting, all those who had any that were sick with various diseases brought them to Him; and He laid His hands on every one of them and healed them (Luke 4:40 NKJV).

> *And the whole multitude sought to touch Him, for power went out from Him and healed them all* (Luke 6:19 NKJV).

> *And Jesus went about all Galilee, teaching in their synagogues, preaching the gospel of the kingdom, and healing all kinds of sickness and all kinds of disease among the people* (Matthew 4:23 NKJV).

> *God anointed Jesus of Nazareth with the Holy Spirit and with power, who went about doing good and healing all who were oppressed by the devil* (Acts 10:38 NKJV).

Jesus is the same yesterday, today, and forever! If Christ was healing yesterday, then He is still healing today, and He wants to do it through your life!

Jesus's assignment to His disciples as well as to us was made clear when He said,

> *And as you go, preach, saying, "The kingdom of heaven is at hand." Heal the sick, cleanse the lepers, raise the dead, cast out demons. Freely you have received, freely give* (Matthew 10:7-8 NKJV).

So we must conclude two things deep within our hearts if we are going to carry glory that manifests miracles. One: it is always God's will to heal. Two: God has commanded us to heal in His name by the power of the Holy Spirit.

WAYS GOD RELEASES HEALING AND MIRACLES

Just as there are ways we receive from God, there are also ways in which God heals and works miracles among us. Again, God's ways will always be connected to His glory.

This chapter is mostly focused on miracles in the glory, which is only one of the ways that He performs miracles. But I also want to share with you other ways in which God performs miracles so you can partner with the Holy Spirit accordingly.

Miracles in the Glory

A few years ago, Miriam and I started to see more and more people supernaturally healed just by being in God's manifest presence. When *the glory* begins to manifest, anything is possible. I would like to suggest that the glory realm is the dimension of accidental miracles. I believe that people will begin to see this more in the days ahead. *The glory* will rest on people in such a way that as they go into the grocery store, those who get within their proximity will suddenly receive supernatural healing and deliverance! Although this dimension of anointing isn't new, according to revival history, it must be believed in and contended for.

Kathryn Kuhlman and Smith Wigglesworth are two great examples of people who walked in such glory that people were healed by the empowering presence of God that overshadowed them. I believe God is looking for people who will dig again the wells of revival and anointing that others have walked in. To confirm this sense from the Lord, He gave me a dream recently that I want to share with you.

Kathryn Kuhlman Phone Call Dream

Recently, I had a dream that Kathryn Kuhlman called me on the phone. After waking from the dream, I asked the Holy Spirit what this could mean. As I continued to ponder and ask the Lord for insight, He revealed to me what it meant and began to share with me that it was a "calling" dream. He said, "I am calling people into the same measure of anointing that Kathryn Kuhlman walked in." That's it! There is a divine invitation from the Father to lay hold of measures of breakthrough that fathers and mothers of the faith previously carried. Mantles, metrons, or measures were never meant to fall to the ground and die with the revivalist who carried them; they were meant to be picked up by succeeding generations.

> *Those from among you shall build the old waste places;*
> *you shall raise up the foundations of former generations;*
> *and you shall be called the Repairer of the Breach, the*
> *Restorer of Streets to Dwell In* (Isaiah 58:12 NKJV).

God is looking for those who are willing to answer the call and go back, apprehending the anointings of previous generations and pulling them into today. Succeeding generations are always meant to sit on the shoulders of previous generations. We are called to move from one realm of glory to the next, not the other way around (see 2 Corinthians 3:18). The anointing that rested on people like Kathryn Kuhlman, Smith Wigglesworth, and others was not meant for just them alone, but for us as well! God is looking for "Repairers of the Breach" who will stand, believe, and contend for greater measures of glory. Let's do this!

I would like to testify to you that "repairs of breaches" are being made! Here are some miraculous healings that Miriam and I have seen in *the glory.* Again, let these testimonies prophesy to you!

Youngsville First Assembly, Lafayette, Louisiana

Tommy, the Sunday morning that you were here, you called a lady up onto the platform who had recently had a surgical procedure on her back. Since the operation, she has had continual pain that has persisted for several months. The surgeon's prognosis was to perform another surgery. Before you even had a chance to lay hands on her, the power of God touched her and she fell out on the floor under God's power. After getting off the floor Sunday morning, she noticed the pain in her back was completely gone! Today, she called the office to report that the pain has not returned and that additional surgery will not be necessary! Let's go, Jesus!

Pastor Joe Cormier

Nicholasville, Kentucky

While ministering with some of our friends in the fields of Kentucky, Miriam and I sensed the Lord was present to heal and release miracles. There were about three thousand people in the field that night, and there was no possible way that we could lay our hands on all of them. As Miriam, myself, and dear friend Ben Hughes released words of knowledge for healing, people began to share with us that God was touching them and they were being healed. I felt that God wanted to heal people with deaf ears, so I called out what I heard in my spirit. As we all prayed for God to miraculously open up deaf ears, over seventy people who were either hearing impaired or completely deaf were healed! No one laid hands on them!

The Deaf Hear! Saturday Night Awakening, Trinity Church

Recently there was a woman who attended our service who was 80 percent hearing impaired in both ears and needed hearing aids to hear. As she was worshiping the Lord, she noticed that her hearing aids didn't seem to work and thought that the batteries needed to be changed. She took them out to put new batteries in and to her surprise she could hear perfectly! She even went out in the lobby to test her ears. She came bringing her hearing aids to us in her hands! She received her miracle by being in the presence of glory! Again, no one laid hands on her!

The Blind See in the Glory!

God continues to release extraordinary miracles everywhere we go. Here is another incredible miracle that happened in the glory, which is mentioned in my wife's book *Glory Miracles*:

> At our Saturday Night Awakening service, one of the most notable miracles was when a teenage boy received sight in his blind eye. We had seen blind eyes healed before, but this story impacts me greatly because God restored more than his eye alone. As a baby, this boy was beaten so severely that he suffered brain damage and lost sight in one of his eyes. His adopted parents saw him through seven surgeries to help correct his eye. This boy was not able to run a few steps without falling down due to brain damage. We always take time to pray for those needing a miracle, and we did so this one particular night. After some were healed, we started transitioning the service to the message, and I heard a gentle nudge of the Holy Spirit say, "I'm not done yet." We had already prayed for miracles, and I had taken my seat. As I prepared to walk out and change my one-year-old's diaper, I felt the gentle nudge in my spirit again. I handed my son to my dear friend Elizabeth and walked back up

on stage. I grabbed a mic and quickly made mention of a healing anointing in the room. Tommy and I decided to wait a little longer in the presence of the Lord. After we called out a few more words of knowledge, a young boy began to run around the front row, then up the steps, onto the stage, and then jump off! He did this two or three times! Tommy was nervous he might trip over the steps because he knew this boy couldn't walk without assistance. But not only was he able to run and jump without falling, but he also began to cry out, "I can see! I can see!" The boy's father came up to report that his son's blind eye had opened; he told the story that led to his son's cognition. No one laid hands on this young man, only the hand of God.[1]

Metal Dissolved! Miami, Florida

While Miriam and I were in Miami ministering at a local church there, we decided it was time to pray for the sick and those needing a miracle. As Miriam and I began to pray for people to receive their healing, one lady began to run back and forth, which caused quite a disruption. The congregation started erupting in praise! Miriam and I looked at each other, wondering what was happening. As the woman began to share her testimony, she stated that she had had an accident years ago and had to have metal surgically implanted in her ankle and part of her shin. The doctors said she would never be able to run again due to the type of fusion that restricted her mobility. She stated that as soon as she heard us say that

God was dissolving metal, she knew she was being healed and began to run! She was able to do things she hadn't been able to do since the surgery!

As she was sharing her testimony, another lady began to jump up and down and started to dance. Again, the congregation erupted in praise to the Lord! She had a similar story—metal surgically implanted in her foot. The doctor said she would never be able to dance again due to lack of mobility and pain. She was instantly healed and was dancing for the first time in years! Both instances happened in the presence of God's glory.

LEVERAGING THE POWER OF THE TESTIMONY

Sharing the testimony of what God has done is a way that we honor the Lord and open up gates of glory. One of the words for *honor* in Hebrew actually is *Kabod,* which of course means "glory." In other words, when we honor the Lord by sharing the testimony, we invite the Spirit of glory to do again what He has done before. As we share the testimony of Jesus, it creates an atmosphere for the King of Glory to come in! Miriam and I have seen countless miracles as we have shared the testimony. In fact, this is how we got started in the healing ministry!

At our very first miracle service, we shared testimonies of what we had seen God do through others because we had not yet experienced miracles ourselves. The testimonies that we shared that night became a gateway of glory! We saw dozens and dozens of healings and creative miracles that night for the very first time! Since then, everywhere we go we make sure to share the testimony of what we have seen God do.

Uber Driver Healed

In one of our weekly gatherings a woman came forward to share that she had been healed all because she heard that God was healing people at our services. My wife, Miriam, shares this testimony in detail in her book *Glory Miracles.*

> One evening in April 2021, my husband and I were leading our Saturday Night Awakening service. We always take time for people to share healing testimonies during our services. A woman came up to share that her body had been healed. When I asked her to share with everyone how Jesus healed her, she mentioned that it was her first time there. She was an Uber driver, and her client invited her to our service. She and her client began to converse about her neurological condition that caused high-level chronic pain that was accompanied by poking sensations on her body. At this, her client gave her a piece of paper. On the paper was written, "Tommy and Miriam Evans" and our service address. Her client said, "If you go to their service, you will be healed. People are being healed there." So she decided to drive an hour and check it out. While sitting in the room, all her pain and the pins and needles sensation completely left! She was overwhelmed by the love of God that day! We don't know who gave her the piece of paper, but we are very thankful God allowed us to be a part of His story.[2]

The testimony of Jesus is the spirit of prophecy (Revelation 19:10 NKJV).

FAITH IN ACTION OPENS UP GLORY GATES

John Wimber, the leader of the Vineyard Movement, once said, "The word *faith* is spelled R-I-S-K." The realm of *risk* is the realm of the miraculous. We have seen hundreds and hundreds of people miraculously healed as they stepped out in faith and took risks to do something that they could not physically do before. Jesus opened up glory gates as He encouraged people to enter the realm of faith through risk to apprehend their much-needed miracle.

> *Then He said to the man, "Stretch out your hand." And he stretched it out, and it was restored as whole as the other* (Matthew 12:13 NKJV).
>
> *I say to you, arise, take up your bed, and go to your house* (Mark 2:11 NKJV).

São José dos Campos, Brazil

Miriam and I were in Brazil, and we were ministering to about two thousand hungry Brazilians who were there with great expectation. We began to call out words of knowledge for healing, and we asked the audience to begin to try and do something that they could not physically do before. A woman in attendance that night was suffering from severe pain and lack of mobility due to an accident she had had that resulted in her getting reconstructive surgery.

The doctors fused her damaged vertebrae together and surgically implanted three metal rods in her back, which caused excruciating pain. This surgical procedure left her with the inability to bend and twist her back. As she heard us encourage the crowd to try and do something that seemed impossible, she decided to bend and twist her back, which again would be physically impossible for her to even do.

As she took a step of faith through risk, her body was instantly healed! When she took a risk in the atmosphere of God's presence, she opened a gate of glory to the creative miracle realm!

LAYING ON OF HANDS DISPENSES GOD'S POWER

Another way that God performs healings and miracles is by the laying on of your hands. Your hands are loaded with anointing! Say this out loud, "My hands are loaded with God's anointing oil to heal the sick and raise the dead!"

Let's look again at the life of Jesus since He is our model for life and ministry.

> *When the sun was setting, all those who had any that were sick with various diseases brought them to Him; and He laid His hands on every one of them and healed them* (Luke 4:40 NKJV).

> *And He laid His hands on her, and immediately she was made straight, and glorified God* (Luke 13:13 NKJV).

Then in Mark's Gospel, Jesus is recorded as saying to the believer:

> *And these signs will follow those who believe: In My name they will cast out demons; they will speak with new tongues; they will take up serpents; and if they drink anything deadly, it will by no means hurt them; they will lay hands on the sick, and they will recover* (Mark 16:17-18 NKJV).

Throughout the years, we have seen many healed by the laying on of hands within our own lives as well as the lives of those we have trained in the ministry of healing and miracles. We encourage people to use common sense when laying hands on people and not to complicate healing prayer by using a lot of technicalities.

For example, if the person that you are praying for has a headache, command the headache to leave in Jesus's name! You don't need to use long, exhausting prayers to get the job done. People are not healed by the length of our prayers but by the finished work of the cross! Simply command whatever it is that they are dealing with to leave and declare healing into the area of the body that needs healing. If a back needs to be straightened, command it to do so. Remember, your hands are loaded with healing power!

WORDS OF KNOWLEDGE CREATE IN THE GLORY

Words of knowledge can be a powerful tool within the hands of the believer. Not only do they have the ability to increase faith for those needing healing, but they also have the ability to activate God's creative miracle power. Paul the apostle referred to words of knowledge as one of the nine gifts of the Spirit when writing to the church in Corinth (see 1 Corinthians 12:8).

A word of knowledge is a *revelation gift* where God will supernaturally download His thought to individuals at specific times to reveal His heart and intention. They will often be specific hidden details about a person's life or need that only God could know. We see this gift regularly in operation in tandem with the prophetic as well as healing. Again, words of knowledge will often bring needed faith for individuals and will also release God's creative power.

So will My word be which goes out of My mouth; it will not return to Me void (useless, without result), without accomplishing what I desire, and without succeeding in the matter for which I sent it (Isaiah 55:11 AMP).

Wow! In other words, when we get a word of knowledge and release it under God's direction, it becomes His words in our mouth that release creative power! And those words will not return to Him void! Come on, Jesus!

Miriam and I have seen many people healed just by releasing words of knowledge in the glory. One such instance was during our Saturday Night Awakening service. Miriam and I were releasing healing prayers and God gave me a word of knowledge that He wanted to heal someone's endocrine system.

As I released the word, there was a woman in the audience who took the word for herself. Two weeks later she confirmed that she was totally healed and was able to get off her medication! After this miraculous healing, this lady continued to drive to our service weekly even though she lived almost two hours away!

I don't know about you, but I feel that it is time that we open up our mouths and watch God fill them with His words! (See Psalm 81:10.) Miracles, healing, and deliverance are in your mouth!

As You Go in Faith Believing

Many times we have found that people have been healed *as they go in faith* after being exposed to God's presence. There may be times when you pray with people and you don't see immediate results. One of the great healing evangelists, Oral Roberts, said that most of the miracles that took place in his ministry actually happened after the meeting was over. People would send in their testimonies sharing that they had received their full healing. In the New Testament, this also happened with ten lepers Jesus prayed for.

> *When He saw them, He said to them, "Go, show yourselves to the priests." And so it was that as they went, they were cleansed* (Luke 17:14 NKJV).

Trigeminal Neuralgia Healed

There was a woman in one of our services who was suffering from a painful and numbing disease called trigeminal neuralgia. She received prayer during one of our Saturday night services without any immediate results. Three days later, she noticed that she was 50 percent better, and by the seventh day every bit of the pain was completely gone!

Tumor Dissolves

Another instance was when a woman responded to a word of knowledge in one of our services, believing for God to dissolve a golf-ball-sized tumor that she had had for over two years. After receiving prayer that night, she woke up the next morning and it was still just as big as it had been the night before. Still standing in faith, she knew that she had received. On the third day as she was getting ready for work, she noticed that the tumor was completely gone! Come on, Jesus!

ANOINTING OIL AND PRAYER CLOTHS

> *Is anyone among you sick? Let him call for the elders of the church, and let them pray over him, anointing him with oil in the name of the Lord. And the prayer of faith will save the sick, and the Lord will raise him up* (James 5:14-15 NKJV).

So many healing revivalists throughout history started to see healings within their ministries when they got the revelation of the supernatural power of the anointing oil that is found in James 5:14-15. Miriam and I have used oil many times while ministering to people and seen several healed this way.

Another way God heals and releases miracles is through prayer cloths and clothing. Again, I don't know how it works, but it works. He's God, so He has the power to do anything. Paul the apostle saw miracles this way.

> *Now God worked unusual miracles by the hands of Paul, so that even handkerchiefs or aprons were brought from his body to the sick, and the diseases left them and the evil spirits went out of them* (Acts 19:11-12 NKJV).

Like Paul, we too have seen God heal people this way as well as set them free. In *Glory Miracles*, Miriam shared one of those instances in detail:

One day I was praying for a gentleman who was standing in proxy for his diabetic, bedridden father. This son explained to me that his father's feet were swollen twice their size, had skin abrasions, and were extremely painful. All I kept hearing was "pray over a handkerchief and send it home to his father." I remembered Acts 19 and the account of Paul's hand cloth being anointed with the Holy Spirit and healing those who touched it. The problem was, I didn't have a handkerchief. I decided I would grab a napkin or piece of paper; I was willing to use anything. I told the gentleman that I had a funny impression about praying over a handkerchief, according to Acts 19. He laughed and said, "This is not funny at all! My dad always carried a handkerchief with him, and he gave one to me and my brother. Now we always carry one!" A burst of deep belly laughter hit the both of us, and we ended up laughing over the handkerchief as we held it in our hands. The gentleman left and took the handkerchief home to his father. A couple weeks later I saw the young man, and he told me that morning after he prayed with his dad and gave him the handkerchief, the swelling in his feet went down and his pain disappeared. He even showed me before-and-after pictures of his dad's feet![3]

One thing I want to add here is that Miriam and I never follow methods—we follow the Holy Spirit. We do our best to hear God's voice and obey. If He tells us to anoint people with oil, then that is what we are doing. If He tells us to call out words of knowledge, then that's what we are doing. Again, relationship with the Holy Spirit and following His leading are the catalytic keys for miracles. Miracles, however they may come, will always be found within His presence.

I will discuss our partnership with angels in the glory realm in the next chapter.

Let's pray together:

Lord, I believe that You have called me to live a life of the miraculous. Lord, I ask that You will activate me with the gift of healing and the working of miracles. Lord, I give You permission to do extraordinary miracles through my life in Jesus's name. Amen.

NOTES

1. Miriam Evans, *Glory Miracles* (Shippensburg, PA: Destiny Image Publishers, 2022).

2. Ibid.

3. Ibid.

CHAPTER 12

Partnering with Angels in the Glory

Are they not all ministering spirits sent forth to
minister for those who will inherit salvation?
—Hebrews 1:14 NKJV

GETTING STARTED

In this chapter, I want to take a little time to discuss with you the importance of our partnership with angels in the advancement of God's Kingdom. This chapter is by no means exhaustive but only serves as a starter chapter that will help you get on the same page with God's agenda as it pertains to the angelic realm. Honestly, it would take a whole new book on the subject to really unpack the topic. Some of what I've pulled together in this chapter is, I feel, probably the most important concerning angels.

WHO TOUCHED ME?

It was my third year of being in the school of ministry at Bethel and I was excited for today's class, because today was the day that Randy Clark was coming to speak to the students. I loved it when Randy came because he always seemed to bring great insight as well as create space for students to really encounter God. Since I was in my third year of the school of ministry, I had the privilege of interning with leaders within the Bethel leadership team to get hands-on experience as well as personal discipleship. I had the wonderful privilege and opportunity to be selected to intern with Pastor Bill Johnson, which came as a great surprise to me. I was like a *needle in a haystack* among about a thousand other students who, in my opinion, were much more qualified and more anointed than me.

Part of my job while interning for Pastor Bill was to assist guest speakers when they came into town to minister. I loved this part of my job because it allowed me to not only personally serve them, but it also allowed me to minister with them as well as learn from them. One of my dear friends and spiritual moms, Deborah Coombs, who oversees all events at Bethel, was actually the one who assigned me to Randy that day.

The room was filled with about twelve hundred hungry first-year students who came with faith-filled expectancy to encounter God. As Randy began to teach on the subject of impartation to the students, the entire atmosphere began to shift and the tangible presence of the Lord filled the room. As Randy discerned the direction of the service, he suddenly decided to jump off the stage into the sea of students to lay hands on all of them to receive impartation. Deborah, who was in charge of the day, looked at me and said, "Go follow Randy and cover him!" Immediately, I took off toward Randy to stand behind him as he walked over chairs and isles to get to expectant students.

As Randy walked through the crowds of students laying hands on them, I followed right behind him laying my hands on students as well. The presence was so strong that I could barely stand to my feet as I walked along following Randy. Every student Randy and I prayed for came under the weighty power of God's presence, falling to the floor encountering God. As we proceeded to lay hands on students, I suddenly felt someone *push* me on my shoulder. I turned around to see who it was and no one was there. The only thing behind me were students lying on the floor encountering God. Again, we continued to lay hands on students, and I felt someone push me on my shoulder a second time. Quickly I turned in hopes of finding out who it was that needed me, but again no one was there. I thought for a moment that I was losing my mind! I kept asking myself, *Who in the world keeps pushing me on my shoulder?* As I pondered who it could be, the presence of God seemed to get even stronger as we ministered.

As we made our way around the room and back toward the side of the stage, I couldn't help but notice that the entire room of students was out under the power of God. No one was left standing! As Randy and I made our way back up the steps and onto the stage, that strong shove came again! Quickly I turned to see who it could be and again no one was there. Then, I heard the Holy Spirit whisper to me, "It's an angel." Through revelation by the Holy Spirit, I began to understand that the reason the angel kept "pushing me" was to get a message from the Lord to me.

As the Holy Spirit gave me more understanding, I realized that God was calling me into the same type of ministry as Randy and He wanted me to know it. The Lord's *push* was His encouragement to me, and He was saying, "You can do this. For I have called you to a ministry of healing, miracles, and impartation." Another thing that the Holy Spirit wanted me to know was that the angel wasn't there just to bring me a message, but he was there to assist Randy and me as we imparted to the students.

OPEN HEAVENS

I would like to propose to you that you carry an open heaven! God gave Jacob, one of the great patriarchs of our faith, a revelation within a dream of what an open heaven looks like:

> *Then he dreamed, and behold, a ladder was set up on the earth, and its top reached to heaven; and there the angels of God were ascending and descending on it. And behold, the Lord stood above it and said: "I am the Lord God of Abraham your father and the God of Isaac; the land on which you lie I will give to you and your descendants"* (Genesis 28:12-13 NKJV).

Later, Jesus prophesied the opening up of the heavens to His disciples:

> *Most assuredly, I say to you, hereafter you shall see heaven open, and the angels of God ascending and descending upon the Son of Man* (John 1:51 NKJV).

When Jesus died on the cross, the veil that separated us from God was torn from top to bottom! That moment on the cross when Jesus said His last words, "It is finished," was the exact moment when the heavens were ripped open! Our precious Jesus has become for us not only the way to the Father, but He also has become the gate and ladder of heaven! In Him, we carry an open heaven where angels ascend and descend upon our lives.

Open heaven is the realm of heaven's activity where God's Kingdom is advanced and angel armies are released. You do not have to pray and beg God to give you an open heaven—you have one! In our book *Decrees that Unlock Heaven's Power*, we have a decree that I think is appropriate in this context. Say this out loud: "I carry an open heaven where angels ascend and descend upon my life, bringing fresh strength, new assignments, and anointing to advance the Kingdom of God."

If this is the position that God has called us to live from, I think it is imperative that the body of Christ have a better understanding of heaven's angel activity.

TWO GUIDING PRINCIPLES FOR ANGELS

As we get started on the topic of angels, there are two things that we must know before we dive into the subject matter. I would encourage you to implement these two things as a plumb line standard to engaging with angels.

> But even if we, or an angel from heaven, preach any
> other gospel to you than what we have preached to you,
> let him be accursed (Galatians 1:8 NKJV).
>
> And no wonder, for even Satan disguises himself as an
> angel of light (2 Corinthians 11:14-15 ESV).

First, if any revelation that you receive from an angelic being does not line up with the revelation that is found in Jesus Christ, *you must discard that revelation.* These types of angels would be considered angels of light or deception.

In his book *The Truth About Angels*, T. Law describes an "angel of light" this way:

> An "angel of light" in biblical terms is not an angel that appears in a burst of light or looks radiant or has a halo around his head. And angel of light, regardless of what he looks like, says, or does, is a spirit who presents a gospel other than what is found in the Bible.[1]

An angel of light, therefore, is one that attracts you with a false gospel. In Randy Clark's book *Entertaining Angels*, he says it this way: "This angel is a messenger from Satan trying to deliver a message of false doctrine."[2] Not only is this the intent, but it has been successful in its mission many times. Both Islam and Mormonism have been biproducts of such an "angelic visitation."

True angels from God will never lead you away from the Lord Jesus or His gospel. They will always promote Jesus and draw you closer to Him. Nor will they try to isolate you from the rest of the body of Christ. If this ever occurs as you interact with them, this is a red flag that you are dealing with an "angel of light" or "angel of deception," which is a demon.

Second, authentic angels from the Lord will never allow you to worship them. See what happened with the apostle John when he encountered an angel:

> *And I fell at his feet to worship him. But he said to me, "See that you do not do that! I am your fellow servant, and of your brethren who have the testimony of Jesus"* (Revelation 19:10 NKJV).

I don't share these things right off the bat so you will become fearful or steer away from engaging with angels. My hope is that by exposing the false you can better recognize the authentic.

ANGELS IN REVIVAL HISTORY

Throughout history, God raised up many revivalists who not only brought revival but also displayed the power of God through signs, wonders, and miracles. I believe that part of their success was because they knew how to leverage the power of the unseen realm through angel armies. William Branham saw thousands miraculously healed, and he attributed that to an angel God had assigned to him.

Many times William would wait to minister healing until he sensed the angel's presence near him. William Branham always promoted Jesus and relied on the Holy Spirit, but he also partnered with his unseen God-given helper.

Another man, by the name of Omar Cabrera, who was a well-known healing evangelist in Argentina who saw thousands upon thousands miraculously healed, also attributed some of his success to his partnership with angels. When Randy Clark was interviewing this South American healing evangelist, Randy asked Omar this question:

> Omar, you are a famous evangelist and I am just getting started and don't know what I am doing. I have just been caught up in this thing and need wisdom. Is there anything you can teach me that would help me where I could see more happening in my meetings?" He looked and said, "Yes." I said, "What?" He said, "Randy, I have never understood why you

North Americans who understand the Holy Spirit, you understand the gifts of the spirit, but why
don't you pray for God to send His angels to your
meetings?"

QUESTION IN MOST CHRISTIANS' MINDS

If we are going to move in realms of God's glory, we need to understand the ministry of angels and their partnership with God as
well as mankind. Like most Christians, I have had these questions
running through my mind for many years: "If God is all powerful,
all knowing, and always present, why do I need angels if I have
that kind of God? Why do I need to partner with angels if I have
Jesus? What about the Holy Spirit and His gifts?"

My study of Scripture as well as reading books written by
others on this subject have really opened up my eyes and have
greatly impacted Miriam's and my ministry. Like others, we too
have seen revival spread, answered prayer, resources unlocked,
divine protection, miracles, healings, deliverance, and glory
released all because we have come to know more fully the importance of partnering with angels. Now, just as God doesn't really
need us to advance His Kingdom, He doesn't need angels either.
However, in His sovereignty He chooses to partner with both
humankind and angels to do mighty exploits. Throughout the
Bible we see Israel referring to God as the Lord of hosts.

Restore us, O Lord God of hosts; cause Your face to shine,
and we shall be saved! (Psalm 80:19 NKJV).

The Hebrew word for *host* is *saba,* which means "host of angels
or company of soldiers." In other words, God is the commander of
angel armies that push back and deal with dark, demonic powers

on behalf of His children! As I pondered and prayed on this subject of angels, the Lord began to tell me that angels and demons (fallen angels) operate in similar ways but have very different assignments toward humankind.

Just like demons can touch people's bodies, inflicting disease, infirmity, and affliction, angels have the ability to touch people, bringing healing, wholeness, and deliverance from those demon powers. It's also the same for those things that can impact our mind, will, and emotions. For instance, just as demons carry an atmosphere of anxiety, fear, torment, suicide, heaviness, and depression, angels carry an atmosphere of joy, peace, love, healing, revelation, healing, and glory. Anytime I sense something that is contrary to the Kingdom of God, I know I'm dealing with a demon spirit.

Now, I never go around looking for a demon or war in the heavenlies, picking fights with demons. I am more interested in what God's angels are doing. I will, however, deal with them when they show up illegally in my home or the worship gatherings that we lead. When they show their ugly heads, I will always ask God to send His holy angels to deal with them or I will bind them in the name of Jesus according to Matthew 16:19, which causes God's mighty angels to respond.

Let's look further at what the Bible says about our partnership with angels.

BIBLICAL BASIS FOR ANGELS

I'll say here again something that I learned from Bill Johnson: "Jesus Christ is perfect theology." Jesus is our model for life and ministry. We see that Jesus too needed assistance from angels, and we see this twice in Scripture. As Jesus was ending His forty-day fast in the wilderness, the Bible says that *"angels came and ministered to Him"* (Matthew 4:11). And again we see an angel come to strengthen Him in the Garden of Gethsemane (see Luke 22:43).

If Jesus needed angelic help, I guess we do too. In addition to these two instances, the New Testament lays the biblical precedent for angelic assistance through the lives of the apostles as well as others. Peter was freed from prison by an angel (see Acts 12:5-7), and an angel told Philip to go to Gaza (see Acts 8:26). While the apostle John was having an open vision, he received angelic assistance for interpretation (see the book of Revelation). When facing shipwreck, Paul the apostle received prophetic insight and encouragement about no one being harmed on the ship (see Acts 27:23). Even a Greek centurion of the Italian Regiment by the name of Cornelius received salvation as well as his entire household, all because of an angelic visitation that led him to invite the apostle Peter to his home.

The bottom line is that we need assistance! As Miriam and I have better understood our need for angelic assistance in both life and ministry, we often will ask God to send angels into the meetings we conduct as well as our home. Because we ask, we have seen new levels of anointing, favor, direction, open doors, protection, and breakthrough for ourselves as well as those to whom we minister.

ANGELIC FUNCTION

As I continued to pray about this subject, the Holy Spirit began to share with me that angels are like "recon marines" in the spirit realm who engage with God, their commanding officer, and make sure His will is accomplished in the earth.

According to the Bible, there are about eight different functions of angels.

Messengers Sent from God

The word for *angel* in Hebrew is *malak*, which means "messenger." In other words, angels bring messages sent from God. We see God sending direct messages to His people through angelic transportation:

- An angel came to Hagar, giving her a message of direction, and prophesied about her son, Ishmael (see Genesis 16:7-13).

- Three angels came to Abraham with a prophetic word about his future and the birth of his son Isaac (see Genesis 18:1-15).

- An angel appeared to Moses in a flame of fire in a bush and spoke to him, giving him a message about God using him to deliver the children of Israel from the hands of Pharaoh (see Exodus 3).

- The mother of Jesus, Mary, was given a message from an angel about her becoming pregnant and giving birth to the Christ (see Luke 1:26).

- Joseph, who was reluctant to take Mary's hand in marriage, received a message in a dream that he should marry her (see Matthew 1:20-24).

- Paul was given a message that no one was going to die even though they were going to be shipwrecked (see Acts 27:23).

- John received revelatory interpretation from an angel (see the book of Revelation).

Angels can come to us in several different ways, according to Scripture. The primary ways in which angels come to us are dreams, open visions, closed visions (visions in your mind), and in person. Also, have you ever seen a sudden flash of light or thought you saw someone out of the corner of your eye? If so, I would like to propose to you that you are in the presence of an angel. When things like this occur, step aside and ask the Holy Spirit to reveal to you why the angels are making themselves known. When you do this, you are acknowledging the Lord, and His promise to you is that He will direct you.

> *In all your ways acknowledge Him, and He shall direct your paths* (Proverbs 3:6 NKJV).

Several years ago, when Miriam and I were living in Redding, I had just finished my first year of ministry school and was contemplating whether I should attend the second-year program. Since the school required a financial commitment as well as time, I was really praying about it. As I fell asleep one night, I had a dream that would give me much-needed direction and insight.

I dreamed that an angel came to me and started to tell me that I was to attend the second-year school of ministry program and that God was going to confirm this word by Miriam becoming pregnant and giving birth to a son. Not long after this dream, we found out that Miriam had become pregnant. After our little discovery, I thought it would be a good idea to go ahead and attend the school! In conclusion to my angelic encounter, nine months later Miriam gave birth to our son Benjamin!

I am so thankful that the Lord sent me an angel to give me this message of direction and prophetic fulfillment. Not only did I receive an incredible son, but when I attended my second year of ministry school, it opened up so many favorable doors that would have never opened for me unless I had been there.

Angels Perform and Respond to God's Word

Psalm 103:20 (NKJV) says, *"Bless the Lord, you His angels, who excel in strength, who do His Word."* Some translations say that His angels "hearken" or "respond" to God's Word. Miriam and I believe so strongly in utilizing the power of decree. I think it would behoove all of us to get the Word of God (the Bible) and start praying the Scriptures! Why? Because God's holy angels respond to it! Maybe this is why we don't see many answers to prayer. Maybe we are praying our will instead of His. Far be it from any of us!

If you don't already have our book *Decrees that Unlock Heaven's Power,* I recommend you get it. It has forty different topics with over two hundred biblically based decrees in it. When we were praying about writing our very first book, God told me, "Give the people what worked for you." When He said this to me, I knew exactly what He meant.

Before Miriam and I saw one miracle or even had a ministry, God inspired us to decree His Word *out loud* over our lives. As we did this, our whole world began to change. Much of what we are currently seeing in our lives and ministry all started because we made a decision to start declaring His promises over our lives, which activates angel armies.

I want to add here a very important note: we must never command angels. Declaring God's promises, asking in prayer, and making petitions release angelic assistance, not our commands. I can, however, command demons to leave because we have been given the authority by Jesus to do so. Just not angels. It is God who commands His angels to come to you (see Psalm 91:11). Again, it is prayer that activates and releases angels. I believe this is the primary way in which we can partner with them.

There are several instances throughout biblical history where we see God intervening by sending angels because someone prayed. King Hezekiah is a great example of what happens in the spirit realm when we pray. An evil, heathen king by the name of Sennacherib was pushing up against God's people and wanted to lay siege to their city. The Bible says that King Sennacherib had a multitude of soldiers ready to destroy Judah.

> *Now because of this King Hezekiah and the prophet Isaiah, the son of Amoz, prayed and cried out to heaven. Then the Lord sent an angel who cut down every mighty man of valor, leader, and captain in the camp of the king of Assyria* (2 Chronicles 32:20-21 NKJV).

If we want angels to ascend and descend upon our lives like they did with Jesus, then we need to start praying and decreeing!

Angels Minister to Heirs of Salvation

> *But to which of the angels has He ever said: "Sit at My right hand, till I make Your enemies Your footstool"? Are they not all ministering spirits sent forth to minister for those who will inherit salvation?* (Hebrews 1:13-14 NKJV).

The Greek word for *minister* is *diakonia*—to serve or to execute the commands of others. In other words, angels come to us under God's command to serve us in life and ministry. They have the ability to serve *to us* what God intends for us to have. If it is provision, they will bring forth that which is needed. If we need joy, strength, a miracle, breakthrough, or help, then that is what they will bring under God's direction. For example, both Jesus and Daniel needed strength while on a fast, and God delivered that strength via angels (see Matthew 4:11; Daniel 10:18).

Angel Brought Provision at Christmas

When Miriam and I lived in Redding, there were times when financially it was a bit tight. I remember one particular year right before Christmas when we could barely rub two pennies together. As a daddy, I really wanted to make sure there were some presents under the tree for my kids on Christmas morning. We just didn't have the means. I remember bringing my concern to the Lord and just resting in His goodness even though it looked like having presents under the tree was not going to happen.

One night while visiting with friends at our house, I suddenly saw two big hands reach up and touch the Christmas ornaments on the back of my tree. At first, I thought one of the kids got back behind the tree, and I quickly got up to see which one of my children it could be. When I looked behind the tree, I realized that all of the kids were upstairs and had not even been down in over an hour! As the ornaments on the tree were still moving back and forth, I quickly asked my friends, "Did you guys see that?" My friend's wife immediately replied, "I did see it!"

We both physically saw with our eyes two big hands reach up and move the Christmas ornaments back and forth on my tree! I realized what had taken place and I suddenly knew that God had sent an angel. Praise God—that ended up being one of the best Christmases we ever had! Christmas presents started showing up in the mail! They kept coming and coming for days. They were even the exact gifts my kids were believing God for! Hallelujah!

In summary, angels are here to minister or serve *to us* all that God has for us. Not only are they here to serve *to us,* but they are also here to serve *with us.* Angels are spirit agents sent from God who minister in the realm of the spirit on our behalf, as well as on behalf of those we minister to.

Angels Give Service and Worship to God

> *Praise Him, all His angels; praise Him, all His hosts!* (Psalm 148:2 NKJV)

Angels love to worship God. This, to me, is another way we can partner with our heavenly allies. Miriam and I make it a point to create an atmosphere of worship within our home. Often, we will turn on worship music and have it playing throughout the house. Sometimes we will let it play during the night as we sleep. Our worship toward God attracts angelic activity.

During one of our weekly revival gatherings, our daughter Kathryn was helping us by leading worship. I remember that the presence of the Lord was so strong that night. We were all lost in God's presence. Kathryn, who often moves prophetically during worship, began to sing about *the glory.* During a time when only the instruments were playing, many of us heard what sounded like angels singing in the background. It was in absolute perfect harmony with the instruments. We went back to watch the recording, and sure enough it was caught on camera!

Angels Transport Our Spirit to Heaven When We Die

Another function of angels is that they transport our spirit to heaven when we die. I have heard of several people who have witnessed angels right before they pass into heaven.

As Jesus was explaining heavenly matters, telling a story about Lazarus and a rich man, He said, *"So it was that the beggar died, and was carried by the angels to Abraham's bosom. The rich man also died and was buried"* (Luke 16:22 NKJV).

Angels Provide Divine protection

Because you have made the Lord, who is my refuge, even the Most High, your dwelling place, no evil shall befall you, nor shall any plague come near your dwelling; for He shall give His angels charge over you, to keep you in all your ways (Psalm 91:9-11 NKJV).

Because you are a child of God, you have access to divine protection! Miriam and I have declared this passage over our family many times. I'm sure all of us can testify that there have been times when you knew you were divinely protected. One such time for me was when I owned an irrigation company and was doing a routine irrigation inspection for one of my clients. As I approached the back side of the property, I began to walk along a rock trail that was next to the water. As I was walking along the trail, I heard one of the loudest internal audible voices I have ever heard say, *"Stop! There is a snake!"* I immediately heard this warning and stopped. As soon as I stopped and waited, a huge venomous cottonmouth snake slithered off the trail and into the water right in front of me! If I had ignored the voice, I would have been bitten for sure.

I want to encourage you, if you ever get some type of directive in your spirit and it doesn't make sense, obey anyway! As long as the word that you are hearing does not violate God's Word, then obey immediately. Joseph the father of Jesus was warned in a dream by an angel to go another way to protect baby Jesus from Herod, who wanted to kill him (see Matthew 2:12-15). Hearing and obeying are key to partnering with angels.

Not only are hearing and obeying imperative for divine protection, but they can also help us when ministering to others. Philip the evangelist was told by an angel to go to Gaza without even knowing his assignment there. When he arrived in Gaza, it was the Holy Spirit who gave him his assignment (see Acts 8:26).

Angels Heal and Perform Miracles

We see in John's Gospel a healing and miracle angel stirring the water at the pool of Bethesda. When the angel would come and stir the water, people would get in and become supernaturally healed.

> *In these lay a great multitude of sick people, blind, lame, paralyzed, waiting for the moving of the water. For an angel went down at a certain time into the pool and stirred up the water; then whoever stepped in first, after the stirring of the water, was made well of whatever disease he had* (John 5:3-4 NKJV).

As mentioned previously, angels are here to serve *to us* as well as *with us*. Miriam and I learned several years ago from Randy Clark the importance of asking God to release His angels during our meetings. We will often ask God to permit His healing and miracle angels to assist us in the realm of the spirit. Every time we have done this, we have seen greater breakthroughs in the area of healing, miracles, and deliverance. As mentioned in Chapter 10, sometimes God will even physically manifest feathers around Miriam and me while we are ministering as a sign to us that His angels are present.

Recently while traveling to Brazil, I had just gotten off a fifteen-hour flight and I was extremely tired because, unfortunately, I am unable to sleep on planes. I had just gotten to my hotel when the inviting organization informed me that I was to minister within one hour. I was physically exhausted! As I arrived at the auditorium full of about 800 hungry students, I realized that I desperately needed God's help to even minister. I kept declaring 2 Corinthians 12:10 over myself: "Your strength is made perfect in my weakness."

As I approached the stage, the presence and power of God came upon me, giving me strength. The glory came and touched all who were there! I asked God to send His healing and miracle angels and began to call out words of knowledge for healing. Several people began to give testimony of their miraculous healing.

One woman stated that as I released healing prayer, she fell under the power of God and onto the floor. As she lay there, she stated that she had a vision of an angel coming and touching her right shoulder that had been in excruciating pain and had been immobile for quite some time. When the angel touched her shoulder, she was instantly healed. We all watched in amazement as she was able to move her arm above her head (*which she could not do before*) and had absolutely no pain!

In Jonathan Nixon's book *Angel Stories,* he shares a testimony given from a healing evangelist by the name of Joan Hunter. Here is her account of the Lord sending angels to assist the working of miracles and healing:

In a service once when I saw an angel for the very first time with my physical eyes, I thought at first I was looking at a cloud, like a glory cloud. I rubbed my eyes, trying to figure it out. I thought, "What is that? Am I having a weird vision, or is this my imagination?" I couldn't really tell. It's like the first time you see something you aren't familiar with. These angels were going over the congregation, over the people in the church, and I was seeing them, but they looked kind of weird to me. And "weird" is really an understatement, but it is the only way I can describe them. These angels didn't have wings; they had an arm span. They were gliding, like flying, over the congregation, and each of them had a big hump on his back. I couldn't figure it out; I couldn't make out what that hump was. It was like I was seeing deformed angels, but I'd never seen or heard of that. Then, suddenly I said, "In the name of Jesus, somebody over here needs a heart. In the name of Jesus I send the word of healing. I send a new heart in Jesus's name." And instantly I saw this angel reach backward into the hump, and at that moment the person I was praying for moved abruptly as if he had been hit by something. In that moment he received a brand-new heart. The humps on the backs of the angels were like backpacks. There were body parts in there! God showed me He had body parts for the people in the service. "This is awesome!" I thought. So I just kept going, and I just kept praying. I saw a man and said, "New lungs," and the angel reached behind into the hump and the man got new lungs! We all saw him react like he'd been hit! He took a really deep breath—haaa—and said, "I can breathe!"[3]

Angels Assist Believers in Starting and Spreading Fires of Revival

You make your angels winds and your servants flames of fire (Psalm 104:4 GW).

Angels are the ones that help administer the fire of God to the lives of people. When God releases revival, He releases His holy flame to ignite people with holy zeal and passion for the Lord. As God releases His holy fire, that fire purges and purifies us, preparing us for His glory.

Isaiah the prophet had a vision that God gave him concerning the glory and the presence of angels:

In the year that King Uzziah died, I saw the Lord sitting on a throne, high and lifted up, and the train of His robe filled the temple. Above it stood seraphim; each one had six wings: with two he covered his face, with two he covered his feet, and with two he flew. And one cried to another and said: "Holy, holy, holy is the Lord of hosts; the whole earth is full of His glory!" (Isaiah 6:1-3 NKJV)

Then one of the seraphim flew to me, having in his hand a live coal which he had taken with the tongs from the altar. And he touched my mouth with it, and said: "Behold, this has touched your lips; your inequity is taken away, and your sin purged" (Isaiah 6:6-7 NKJV).

The term *seraphim* is plural for the word *seraph*, which means "burning one." James Goll describes it this way when talking about the seraphim:

> The seraphim cry "holy, holy, holy" to each other all the time—and they bring purity to sinful human beings so that we can approach the throne of God. I think that when we experience the manifest presence of God and feel utterly undone and small, the seraphim have been released to come into our realm.[4]

PROXIMITY

In summary, praying, declaring the Word, hearing and obeying, asking the Holy Spirit to send help, and worshiping are things that we can do to activate and initiate a partnership with angels. In addition to these, I want to include one other way in which we can partner with angels. I am referring to *close proximity*. When I see, discern, or feel an angel, I will try to get into close proximity to the angel. For instance, when I see, discern, or feel one, I will go and stand next to it while asking the Holy Spirit how I need to partner with that angelic being.

Recently, I had a vision of an angel appearing in front of the door of my home. When I asked the Holy Spirit what kind of angel it was and what I needed to do to partner with it, I heard the angel say to me, "I am a watcher angel who watches over the doorway to the spirit realm over your family." He went on to tell me, "I allow what God wants in and I disallow what is not allowed by God. I also open up new doors and close old ones." Suddenly I felt that I was to walk over to my door and stand next to the angel and prophesy to my front door as a prophetic act.

As I was releasing the prophetic decree, the angel was opening up new doors and closing old ones. I felt a much-needed shift in the atmosphere over my home as I partnered with the angel God had sent.

There also have been times in our services when an angelic presence will reside in one area of the room and you can tangibly feel it. Often, I will encourage people to go to the area where I sense the angel is standing and see what happens. Every time we have done this, people can barely stand on their feet as they approach the area. Other times an angel will come into the room and stand in a specific spot releasing the *oil of joy.* When people get in close proximity, they begin to get intoxicated with joy through holy laughter. It has been the same with healing and miracles as well. I believe that Miriam and I have healing and miracle angels that minister with us regularly because this is a primary function of our ministry. At times, Miriam and I can tangibly feel a healing angel ministering with us as we minister healing to others.

Whether you are moving in healing, praying, preaching the gospel, or prophecy, I want to encourage you to ask God to send His angels to assist you. Remember, when they show up to assist, ask the Holy Spirit how you can partner with them to advance the Kingdom.

Let's pray:

> *Thank You, God, that You are the Lord of hosts. Thank You for sending angels to assist me as well as minister to me when needed. Holy Spirit, I invite You to guide me through every angelic encounter that I may have. May*

Your angels ascend and descend upon my life so that Your Kingdom can be advanced through me. Amen.

NOTES

1. T. Law, *The Truth About Angels* (Orlando, FL: Creation House, 1994), 30.

2. Randy Clark, *Entertaining Angels* (Apostolic Network of Global Awakening, 2008), 59.

3. Jonathan Nixon, *Angel Stories* (Lake Mary, FL: Charisma House, 2014), 13-14.

4. James Goll, *Angelic Encounters* (Lake Mary, FL: Charisma House, 2007), 59.

CHAPTER 13

JOY UNSPEAKABLE AND FULL OF GLORY

Though now you do not see Him, yet believing, you
rejoice with joy inexpressible and full of glory, receiving
the end of your faith—the salvation of your souls.
—1 PETER 1:8 NKJV

During my second year in ministry school, I had the incredible opportunity to travel with one of my spiritual mothers, Deborah Coombs, with some other students to Asia for two weeks. A few days before I was about to leave, I came down with a horrible case of the flu. I remember calling Deborah the night before, thinking that it might be a good idea if I just canceled. She encouraged me to not give up hope and to meet her at the airport even though I was

feeling quite horrible. When I got to the airport, I used every bit of strength I had just to check in my bag and get to the terminal gate. I thought to myself, *This is absolutely stupid,* and kept questioning why I was even going when I felt so bad.

As I sat across the room trying to keep my distance from the rest of the team, Deborah made a beeline to me. I could see her coming straight for me with her big, intense blue eyes and knew that she was ready to deal with whatever it was that I was dealing with physically. As soon as she got to me, she grabbed my hands and just stared at me for what seemed like forever. It was quite uncomfortable, to say the least.

Not only was she in my personal space, but she just kept staring at me with a pretty intense look on her face. All of a sudden, out of nowhere, Deborah began to laugh out loud as she continued to look at me with intensity! I was thinking, *What has gotten into the lady? I think she has lost her mind!* As she continued to laugh out loud while staring directly at me, suddenly laughter hit me. I could not have helped myself if I had wanted to! I was undone! Deborah and I continued to laugh hysterically for at least seven to ten minutes, then, just as quickly as it came, it stopped. As I stepped onto the plane, I couldn't help but notice that some of the discomfort that I had been dealing with had begun to leave. By the time I landed in Beijing, China, I was totally healed! I was healed by an impartation of joy through holy laughter!

HEAVEN'S AMBASSADORS

I believe that one of the vehicles that God is using to release His glory in these last days is *heaven's joy* through holy laughter! Unfortunately, because this manifestation of the Spirit is so misunderstood, it is often rejected by much of the church. The Bible and revival history are full of truths concerning the connection between *the glory* and joy. I believe it is time for the church to get a greater revelation on leveraging the supernatural power of joy. Like I said in an earlier chapter, if we are going to move into new realms of God's glory, then we have got to be okay with the ways in which God manifests despite our misunderstanding of it. As glory carriers, you and I become carriers of the atmosphere of heaven, and angels ascend and descend upon us. We become an open gate of glory where signs, wonders, and miracles manifest, causing the sick to be healed and the demonized to be set free.

As heaven's ambassadors, we represent the Kingdom of God legislating from heaven's perspective as well as its activity. There is no sickness, depression, anxiety, or depression in heaven, so as ambassadors our job is to make sure that those things are not represented here. When teaching His disciples to pray, Jesus taught them, *"On earth as it is in heaven."* If it doesn't exist in heaven, then it must not be allowed to exist here. As gatekeepers to the heavenly realm, we not only become catalysts for miracles, healings, and freedom, but we also become catalysts for heaven's joy.

Joy is so valuable to God that He actually made it one of the pillars of the Kingdom. According to Scripture, *joy* is actually one third of the Kingdom! When addressing the church in Rome, Paul said, *"For the kingdom of God is not a matter of eating and drinking, but of righteousness, peace and* joy *in the Holy Spirit"* (Romans 14:17 NIV). If this is the case, then we must make room for ourselves and others to encounter this incredible gift of abundant joy.

THE SUPERNATURAL POWER OF JOY

As glory carriers, we must know that if the enemy of our souls can steal our joy, then he can stop the flow of our anointing. The enemy doesn't mind someone who preaches well or sings well, but he is terrified of someone who carries the anointing. This is why he will do whatever he can to steal our joy, because he knows it is the source of our strength and the gate that keeps the anointing flowing in our lives. This is why we must do whatever it takes to protect it by continuing to feast upon the Lord's joy. We do this by staying continuously connected to His presence. *"In Your presence is fullness of joy; at your right hand are pleasures forevermore"* (Psalm 16:11 NKJV).

Heaven's joy is the strength and protection of the anointing. Joy has the ability to cover us and keep us in a state of overflow as well as progressing forward in life. When Israel was getting some resistance from their enemies while rebuilding the walls of Jerusalem, Nehemiah encouraged them by saying, *"Do not sorrow, for the joy of the Lord is your strength"* (Nehemiah 8:10 NKJV). Joy is the very thing that empowers us with God's strength to fulfill our God-given assignments.

IMPARTATION OF JOY

Most often, when God imparts His supernatural joy in your life, He will impart it to you through *holy laughter.* I have seen countless people set free from years of depression, heaviness, anxiety, and even receive supernatural healing via joy through *holy laughter.* God's supernatural joy is a powerful weapon that has the ability to dismantle and displace powers of darkness over people, cities, and even nations. One ounce of heaven's joy can do for you what years of counseling could never do. I am all for counseling; it has its place, but I sincerely believe it pales in comparison.

A few years ago, Miriam and I were in northern Brazil on a missionary assignment that God had given us to minister to about two hundred pastors in the region. It was my turn to speak, and I wasn't quite sure what God had in mind. As worship continued, suddenly the heavy glory came in the room, touching all who were present. I remember when God came upon us, we were overwhelmed by God's intense love, and I could do nothing else but lie prostrate on my face. I wept and wept, for God was again doing a deep work in me. Anytime I am about to minister, I always ask God to give me His fresh anointing for my life so I have something fresh to give away. I know that anything that comes to me is meant to go through me and back to God. That's just the way it works.

After getting off the floor, I still had no idea what God wanted to do. So I just began to talk about God's amazing love. As I walked by the front row, I looked directly at one of the pastors and stuck out my hand toward him. As I stuck out my hand, he immediately took hold of it and jumped up, shouting and laughing uncontrollably! As the glory continued to rest upon this man, he apparently was unable to stand anymore, so he fell forward toward me and I quickly had to step aside so he wouldn't take me down with him!

As this pastor lay there, he continued to laugh and laugh uncontrollably, which led others in the room to catch what he had caught from the Lord. Before I knew it, the whole place was hit with laughter! No one could help themselves! The whole room had erupted in exuberant laughter! God was in the room and He was handing out what every one of those pastors needed!

I wasn't even going to think about touching this! It was God and everyone knew it! One of the keys to moving in the glory is to move with it when it begins to manifest. We must never quench the Spirit of God. When He starts to move, that's when we must yield and move with Him or get out of the way!

Later that day, I found out that the pastor who had been blasted by God's joy was actually put on a mandatory six-month sabbatical by his primary care physician because of physical exhaustion due to stress and clinical depression. His doctor told him if he didn't take a sabbatical, the stresses of the ministry could kill him. After his encounter with God's joy that morning, he reported that God delivered him from years of depression. He went on to testify that all the depression had left him in an instant. He said he hadn't felt that light in years. In about sixty seconds, through the oil of joy, God destroyed the yoke of depression and stress that this pastor had been carrying for years! He went back to his hometown and continued in the ministry and is still doing a mighty work for God to this day! Come on, Jesus! His ways are higher than our ways, and His thoughts are higher than ours!

Joy through laughter is supernatural, and our finite minds will not always understand it. It is a thing of the spirit and must be spiritually discerned. Earthbound logic cannot comprehend the things of the Spirit; only a heavenly mindset can do so. It is high time for all of us to get on the same page with heaven and let God renew our minds according to the pattern of heaven! If we are going to step into the new things that God has for us, then we must be willing to go places in God that we may not fully understand. Think about it—if we could figure all of this out, then God wouldn't be God. The God of joy wants us to embrace all that He has for us! If we are going to embrace things like His abundant joy, then we must understand that it will require faith to embrace it, not our understanding.

GOD LAUGHS

Not only did God create joy through laughter, but the Bible even records God laughing Himself: *"The One enthroned in heaven laughs"* (Psalm 2:4 NIV). The Bible says that Jesus was anointed with the oil of joy far above His companions (see Hebrews 1:9). Jesus was attractive to a lost and dying world not only because of His love but also because of His joy.

If our Lord is laughing, then I think it is high time for His church to start! It has always been a quandary to me why laughter within church gatherings is so offensive to so many. And we wonder why the lost want nothing to do with us. Why in the world are all of our church services so serious and somber? If I remember correctly, "seriousness" is not a fruit of the Holy Spirit! Instead of being so serious and somber, why not laugh a little in our gatherings? Why not let God move how He wants to and let Him deliver to us what He knows we need the most.

JOY THROUGH LAUGHTER RELEASES HEALING POWER

Abundant joy in the life of a believer not only attracts the lost, but it also can bring healing to those in need. *"A joyful heart is good medicine, but a crushed spirit dries up the bones"* (Proverbs 17:22 ESV). Miriam and I have seen this time and time again. Anytime God begins to pour out the oil of joy in a service, it will most often result in people getting physically and emotionally healed.

Recently Miriam and I had the wonderful opportunity to appear on *The Jim Bakker Show* in Blue Eye, Missouri. Along with appearing on the show, we had the privilege to be able to minister to the retired church community there. It was my turn to minister, and the only thing that I knew God wanted me to do was to preach out of 1 Thessalonians 5. As I began to preach, a lady in the front row began to laugh hysterically and apparently was not able to contain herself.

Suddenly, others in the room began to laugh as well, and before I knew it the whole congregation was hit with a wave of joy through holy laughter! I honestly didn't know what to do at first, so I just invited them to come to the front. As they approached the stage one by one, they began to fall under the power of God and were laughing hysterically on the floor. I saw a ninety-five-year-old man holding back tears of joy as he *belly laughed* out loud while another lady in a wheelchair was bent over laughing without constraint. To be honest, it was a sight to see. As I watched God pour out the oil of joy on this little retirement community, I too became intoxicated with joy! I was undone! I was finished! God was there and everyone in the room knew it!

Later, after the service, it became evident why God was pouring out His joy on this little retirement community. One by one, people began to share testimonies of how God had healed their broken heart with His joy. It became apparent to me that many in the room had experienced the loss of a loved one the previous year and were dealing with depression because of it. One woman came to me in tears and said to me, "I haven't laughed like this since I lost my son Johnny a year ago." Another woman came to me and said that she had been depressed since she had lost her husband several months back and reported that she was totally free from depression and felt a sense of purpose again. The joy of the Lord carries healing power!

JOY IN GOD'S PRESENCE

I believe as glory carries we can live in a continuous joy that releases the glory of God everywhere we go. It's in God's presence that our joy is complete and made full. When my children were babies, anytime I would reach down and get in their face they would always smile. In the Bible, the meaning for the word *presence* is "face." So when Psalm 16:11 (NKJV) states, *"In Your presence is fullness of joy,"* it's saying, "In God's face there is fullness of joy." When you and I get in our heavenly Father's face, it puts a smile on ours! As we learn to carry and host the presence of the Lord, our countenance changes and begins to reflect the countenance of the Lord Jesus, revealing His beauty.

ARISE AND SHINE

As I close this book, I want to leave you with something that is really burning in my spirit for you. God has chosen you to arise, shine, and carry His glory! He is calling you and commissioning you right now! Jesus came as the light of the world, and then He passed the baton off to you and me, saying, *"You are the light of the world"* (Matthew 5:14 NKJV). As we behold the Lord, we become the very image of the one and only Jesus! We have become His exact representation in the earth! We are image bearers of light in the darkness! Now is the time for you and me to arise and shine to a lost and dying world so that Jesus can get His full reward. You were born for such a time as this!

Arise, shine; for your light has come! And the glory of the Lord is risen upon you. For behold, the darkness shall cover the earth, and deep darkness the people; but the Lord will arise over you, and His glory will be seen upon you. The Gentiles shall come to your light, and kings to the brightness of your rising (Isaiah 60:1-3 NKJV).

You are the light of the world. A city that is set on a hill cannot be hidden. Nor do they light a lamp and put it under a basket, but on a lampstand, and it gives light to all who are in the house. Let your light so shine before men, that they may see your good works and glorify your Father in heaven (Matthew 5:14-16 NKJV).

CLOSING PRAYER

Lord, thank You that my joy is complete within Your presence. Thank You for anointing me to carry Your glory on the earth. Teach me, Holy Spirit, how to do life with You and lean into all that You have for me. Teach me Your ways, oh Lord, so that I may carry Your beauty and reflect Your life wherever I might go. Come now, Lord, and multiply Your anointing so that I may bring You honor and glory in Jesus's name. Amen.

About Tommy Evans

Tommy Evans is a revivalist who burns to see revival fires spread throughout the earth. Tommy travels locally, nationally, and internationally holding revival gatherings, miracle services, and supernatural school intensives. Tommy and his wife, Miriam, are the founders of Revival Mandate International, whose mission is to see Jesus glorified through the power of the Holy Spirit.

Tommy and Miriam have co-authored a book, *Decrees that Unlock Heaven's Power for Miracles*. They have made guest appearances on Sid Roth's *It's Supernatural!*, *The Resting Place*, and *The Jim Bakker Show*. Both Miriam and Tommy are members of the Apostolic Council of Prophetic Elders with Generals International.

Tommy, Miriam, and their five children live in the Dallas/Fort Worth, Texas, area.

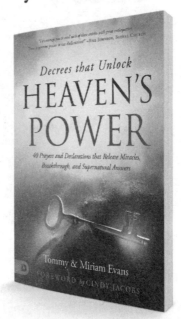

From
Miriam Evans

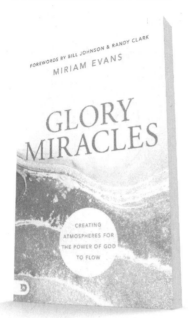

Miracles, signs, and wonders can be part of your everyday life!

When you study the life and ministry of Jesus, it becomes quickly evident that miracles are central to the Gospel. Miracles are demonstrations of God's supernatural power that draw people to Himself!

As a follower of Jesus, you have been anointed and commissioned to move in the same kind of miraculous power as Him! Whether you are a teacher, doctor, lawyer, government official, pastor, or a homemaker; as a child of God, it is your inheritance to live in supernatural healing and bring it to those who need it! In *Glory Miracles*, author and healing evangelist, Miriam Evans shows you how.

By creating atmospheres that welcome God's glory, you can *personally* heal the sick, raise the dead, cast out demons, and operate in the miraculous. You don't need a minister, church, or special healing evangelist to do this! This is God's will for *you*.

Filled with sound Scriptural teaching and compelling testimonies from modern-day miracles and healing revivalists of old, *Glory Miracles* will provoke you to enter new realms of Holy Spirit demonstration and encounter!

Purchase your copy wherever books are sold

From
Cindy Jacobs

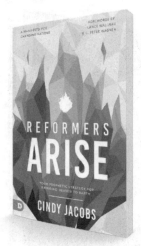

This is your prophetic commissioning!

In these last days, the prophets foresee a great Holy Spirit out-pouring – a revival that will not be constrained by the four walls of an institution, but will shake the whole earth, shifting the very landscape of nations. This book is your prophetic commission-ing to take your place in God's imminent plan for mighty revival!

Cindy Jacobs is a renowned prophet to the nations with a heart that burns for revival and reformation. In this timely work, she steps into her office as a prophetic general, calling revived be-lievers to take their place as supernaturally-empowered agents for societal change.

In this freshly updated edition of her landmark book, *Reforma-tion Manifesto,* Cindy provides two new chapters that give pro-phetic insight on the present revival, coming awakening, and the great reformation that will see moves of God become societal transformation.

Rise up! It's time to take your place in Heaven's agenda for the world!

Purchase your copy wherever books are sold

From

Bill Johnson

Experience Continuous Revival

Historically there have been seasons where Gods presence awakens revival moving in powerful ways, saving souls, and releasing miracles. We often think of these seasons as isolated, unique outpourings of the Spirit.

Is it possible to experience revival every day, as a way of life?

Pastor Bill Johnson answers with a resounding Yes!

Globally recognized bestselling author, and senior leader of Bethel Church in Redding, CA, Bill Johnson is a revivalist at heart. In his time at Bethel, the church community has experienced what can only be called a perpetual, continuous outpouring of the Holy Spirit.

In this landmark book, pastor Bill teaches from his experience as the shepherd of this movement, imparting his own passion for revival along with practical wisdom for sustaining a move of God on both a personal and corporate level.

If you are hungry for a fresh move of God in your life, church, or community, *Open Heavens* will guide you through preparing the altar, encountering the fire of God, and keeping it burning every day! Why settle for anything less?

Purchase your copy wherever books are sold

From

Patricia King

Prophetic Strategies and Warnings for the Next 10 Years

At the inauguration of the year 2020, Christian prophets unanimously recognized that the Church was not merely entering a new year or season, but an entirely new era. To align with God and His purposes for this new era, it is vital that every Christian is aware of God's directives, so they can move in sync with His Spirit in the coming days.

In *A Prophetic Manifesto for the New Era*, globally recognized prophet and bestselling author Patricia King offers a prophetic plumb line—a prescient standard for believers to walk in Kingdom success.

Uniquely presented through short, reflective readings, with accompanying prayers of activation and devotional insights, Patricia shares how to walk vigilantly and victoriously in this new era.

Includes prophetic words on...

·Cultural reformation ·Increased supernatural visitation · Escalated miracles · The fear of the Lord · The call to consecration · A breakthrough era · The days of awe · Great shakings: wars, rumors of wars, natural disasters, and plagues · Divine wisdom and the counsel of God

Don't be blind to the season you are living in! Discover God's word for this era, and start walking in His eternal purposes!

Purchase your copy wherever books are sold

YOUR *Prophetic* COMMUNITY

Sign up for **FREE** Subscription to the Destiny Image digital magazine, and get awesome content delivered directly to your inbox!

destinyimage.com/signup

Sign-up for Cutting-Edge Messages that Supernaturally Empower You

- Gain valuable insights and guidance based on biblical principles
- Deepen your faith and understanding of God's plan for your life
- Receive regular updates and prophetic messages
- Connect with a community of believers who share your values and beliefs

Experience Fresh Video Content that Strengthens Your Prophetic Inheritance

- Receive prophetic messages and insights
- Connect with a powerful tool for spiritual growth and development
- Stay connected and inspired on your faith journey

Listen to Powerful Podcasts that Equips You for God's Presence Everyday

- Deepen your understanding of God's prophetic assignment
- Experience God's revival power throughout your day
- Learn how to grow spiritually in your walk with God

In the Right Hands, This Book Will Change Lives!

Most of the people who need this message will not be looking for this book. To change their lives, you need to **put a copy of this book in their hands.**

Our ministry is constantly seeking methods to find the people who need this anointed message to change their lives. **Will you help us reach these people?**

Extend this ministry by sowing 3 books, 5 books, 10 books, or more today, and become a life changer! Your generosity will be part of catalyzing the Great Awakening that many have been prophesying and praying for.